AuthorHouse™
1663 Liberty Drive
Bloomington, IN 47403
www.authorhouse.com
Phone: 833-262-8899

Because of the dynamic nature of the Internet, any web addresses or links contained in this book may have changed
since publication and may no longer be valid. The views expressed in this work are solely those of the author and do
not necessarily reflect the views of the publisher, and the publisher hereby disclaims any responsibility for them.

Any people depicted in stock imagery provided by Getty Images are models,
and such images are being used for illustrative purposes only.
Certain stock imagery © Getty Images.

This book is printed on acid-free paper.

ISBN: 978-1-7283-4890-2 (sc)
ISBN: 978-1-7283-4891-9 (e)

Library of Congress Control Number: 2020904123

Print information available on the last page.

Published by AuthorHouse 03/03/2020

authorHOUSE

EXCURSIONS
of the
MIND²

stories take flight

JOANNE KENZY

POEMS

Welcome to
My World of Words

HOPE TO HORROR TO HEALING

LATIN LOVE

CASCADING MOMENTS

DAVID'S DANCE

CLARK KENT

DANUBE BLUE

THROUGH DREAMS

THE KISS

WALES BEYOND WALES

TREE OF LOVE

CANYONS OF THE WORLD

LET FREEDOM RING

ENCHANTMENTS BY GOD

GIRL OF HIS DREAM

FEARS

FREEDOM FOR A NEW LAND

HEAVENLY LIBRARY

GOODRICH GHOSTS

LOVE AFFAIR

OCEANS

HARVEST TIME

ORIGINAL BOND

MAJESTIC MESSAGES

SONG OF THE HEART

WINGS

CRYING EAGLE

YOUR DESTINY

FAKE NEWS

CHICAGO HEAT

CORRUPTION

FROZEN IN TIME

EYES ON THE PRIZE

SHADOW LOVE

TWILIGHT'S LAST GLEAMING

VALENTINE LOVE

THE GARDEN

BOW TO BACH

LAND OF THE DEAD

NORTH POND HERMIT

SEASONS OF SUMMER

SONG OF CREATION

SUNKEN CITY

Invisible Ink

Images that form on paper
A temporal explosion or a kiss of a rhyme
Pent-up thoughts bursting out
The pen releases a story from time

The powers of that inner cantata
Shaping my thoughts by embracing the years
Invisible ink now seen on paper
Touched by my soul and sometimes my tears

Words lighting fires in the minds of men
Trying to say what I feel; what I love
Breaking through the shackles of time
Absorbing the words that fall from above

Welcome to voices heard in my world
Words that create powerful spells
Words that shape a world in ink
Giving cause to a soul & the power to think

Peace and love

Harmony

The cadence of the universe
The dance of harmony
Perfect notes merging as one
Songs of love being sung

At the center of who we are
We seek to walk in harmony
Follow the song as it sings
Enjoy the peace that it brings

Life giving forces guide our steps
All that matters to you and I
Trying to create heaven on earth
While grabbing lost chords from out of the sky

FOLLOWING THE

The cry of a broken heart
The travail of a stricken soul
Revealing her broken, invisible life
Now becoming a life-driven goal

Escaping the monsters of North Korea
Fearful and alone
She steals her way to another land
The unchanging desert with Gobi sand

Great sands glowing gold
Beneath the stark blue sky
A shattered life she did not choose
As she walks, she wonders why

STARS

The night arrives, dressed in purple
Motionless now she stares
Filling her eyes with the universe
Millions of stars are now hers

A messenger sent by God
A living epitaph
Exposing a country filled with scars
One brave woman who followed the stars

Thank you, Yeonmi Park, who escaped North Korea

DANCING
in the
Park

They agreed to meet
In Central Park
At a bench in the courtyard
Just before dark
An orchestra is playing
At the nearby square
Musical rhythms are filling the air
She rose, extending her hand
Took a rhythmic step and swayed
Seeing the satin come to life

He mirrored the lunges done by this maid
Expressing now what is too deep for words
Their dancing turns into ecstasy
A speechless meeting has just taken place
In a courtyard beneath the old staircase

Venice

A tongue of land
Shuts off the lagoons
Divides them from the sea
Ebb and flow
Land and tide
Swelling, cresting, having to be

Deep canals run through the marshes
The highways of this city
A kaleidoscope of colors mirrored
Lapping the walls of history

Artists of the floating world
Ply their long-painted oar
Lighted torches fixed on poles
Melodies heard while sensations soar

Tunes adapted to little poems
Sung by gondoliers
Penetrating voices can be heard
Echoing from these balladeers

Unforgettable romantic ambiance
Passing under the Bridge of Sighs
On this highway in the heart of Venice
The sun drops sparks from the sky

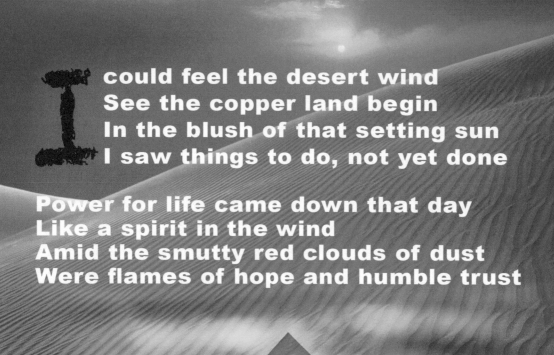

I could feel the desert wind
See the copper land begin
In the blush of that setting sun
I saw things to do, not yet done

Power for life came down that day
Like a spirit in the wind
Amid the smutty red clouds of dust
Were flames of hope and humble trust

DESERT WINDS

I stepped into His destiny
With ambient words inside of me
"I know the plans I have for you
Things that no one else can do"

Sitting between heaven and earth
Hearing His will unfold
I knelt down in humble prayer
While the desert winds filled the air

ALL ROADS LEAD

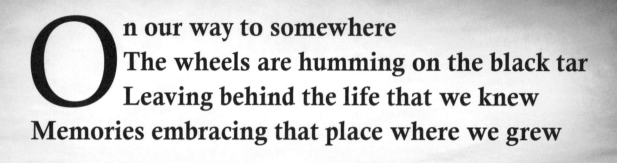

On our way to somewhere
The wheels are humming on the black tar
Leaving behind the life that we knew
Memories embracing that place where we grew

TO SOMEWHERE

Sometimes unendurably bumpy
The road unfurls before us
Yesterdays are all that we know
There are signs on the road to see as we grow

Where the road meets a road and the road has a bend
We make the decision, so the road does not end
We bend with the curve, pick the one we think right
Avoiding the road leading into the night

ANOTHER TIME

From the window of the breakfast-room
While nursing the morning coffee
She sees branches bended low
Covered with ice and new-fallen snow

The view is strangely magical
Feelings of wonder, a world transformed
Then she feels the room pull away
Taking her back to a bygone day

Now harboring this fantasy
She walks amid a snow-globe world
Feels the white pearls of love
Descending from the heavens above

The streets are silent, all draped in white
White smoke rises from chimneys in sight
After all these years of being away
The scene is a picture of just yesterday

Glimpses and flashes of snow flurries blowing
Views from a storybook loved as a child
All here is peaceful and still
As she sits in the chair in front of the sill

Winter was fading here on the plains
The temperatures were high for the time
Then the winds began to blow
Bringing the rain; then new-falling snow
Little by little the temperatures dropped
Plunging into cold, cold, cold

BLIZZARD ON THE PLAINS

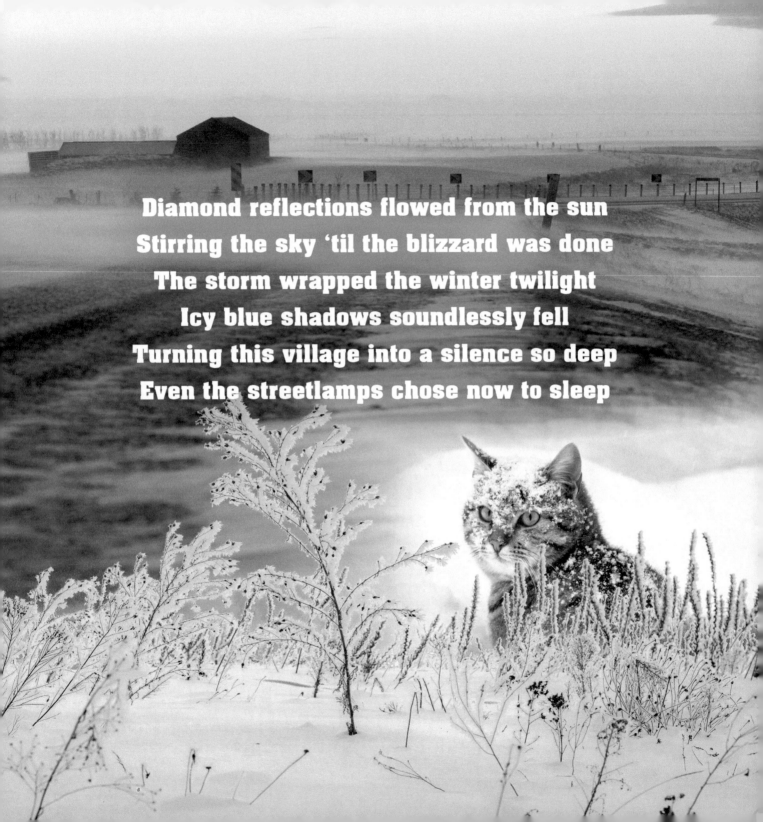

Diamond reflections flowed from the sun
Stirring the sky 'til the blizzard was done
The storm wrapped the winter twilight
Icy blue shadows soundlessly fell
Turning this village into a silence so deep
Even the streetlamps chose now to sleep

BIRTH OF THE

The splendor of Itasca
Holding countless lakes and bogs
Towering forests of red and white pine
Visitors' cabins made from the logs

Black bears live on Wilderness Drive
Loons and herons wade in the lakes
Owls, woodpeckers and finches
Add to sounds that the forest makes

MIGHTY MISSISSIPPI

Transparent water, flowing free
Leaving mounds and depressions for us to see
Smelling the sharp, pungent trees
Stepping a stream beneath their canopy

Headwaters of the mighty Mississippi
The remains of a giant ice-flow
Winding southward from this lake
Into the Gulf of Mexico

Message to
KING GEORGE

The bell-man ascended the steeple
He leaned against the wall
A little boy was placed at the door
The door to Independence Hall!

That old bell-man waited long
"Will they ever do it?" he kept saying
And while he waited in that stall
That old man knelt and he was praying

AMERICA

"Give liberty to this land
And to the inhabitants thereof;
That taxation and representation are inseparable
Give us the freedom that we love"

Suddenly a loud shout arose from below
The blue-eyed boy yelling "Ring, let her ring"
The Declaration of Independence had just been signed
And with purity of purpose was sent to the king!

BORN IN

BARCELONA

I have come alive
Rising through forgotten books
A witness steeped in history
Stepping out of ancient nooks

I wander through the cobblestone streets
Midst the buildings leaning tall
Hidden courtyards, winding alleys
Seeing remains of a Roman wall

Born in that place where history unfolds
I find myself amid shuffling feet
Stopping to share my stories
With throngs of visitors I find on the street

Now beneath the Gothic arch
I am standing at the heart
A Bridge of Sighs from long ago
When counts and kings dodged the dart

Here on Barri Gotic streets
In beautiful Barcelona Spain
Tourists fill the arty bars
While learning of those wars of gain

Picasso's early stomping ground
Hemingway's favorite haunt
I welcome you to come and feel
Visions direct from history's reel

CoLD, So CoLD

Coming forward through the snow
Forgotten faces she used to know
Filling now vacant spaces
In that town from long ago

When she becomes a child again
Magic becomes a wand
Stirring the wonder of her youth
Spreading visions of wisdom and truth

Amongst the snowdrifts lying there
Stands a church, cold and bare
One where no church-bell rings
One where no choir sings

Echoes in those vacant places
Voices with hymns she used to sing
Through those eyes with dreams to bring
The snow is wrapping everything

In those cold, quiet hours
In a cold, quiet place
She has memories to embrace
Memories that age cannot erase

QUIVERING SOUNDS

Slipping away from a busy world
On this moonlit night
Gently caressed by a memory
You, me, the winds and the sea

Hearing rhythms painted on silence
Echoes from a Bossa Nova band
Moody chords quivering down
Touching the waves and the ivory sand

A lyrical fusion of samba and jazz
Sounds that you can see
Touched by the magic Moved by the strings
Feeling the sway of just you and me

Sounds reverberating to the stars
Acoustics played on nylon guitars
Marimbas making the music speak
While I feel your breath caressing my cheek

THORNS AND THISTLES

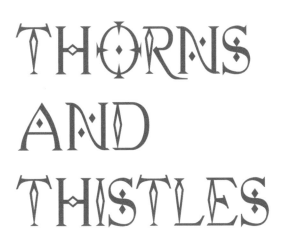

Thorns and thistles, on the life-path we tread
Thorns and thistles, a touch that we dread
A path that we travel, though rough winds blow
Through a life here on Earth, that we do not know

God said long ago
Through these places you will go
You will eat by the sweat of your brow
For you do not live in my garden now

Eden's curse became a mocking crown
The crown of thorns that Jesus wore
Thorns woven into a beautiful plan
By the obedient One with salvation for man

HOME OF

Below the government building
In "de basement" where I live
I yearn to be precious and cherished
Not have my beauty drained like a sieve

After many years of growing older
My dress has gotten thin and thinner
Some guys came in and took me out
Saying we were having dinner

PENNY NICKELS

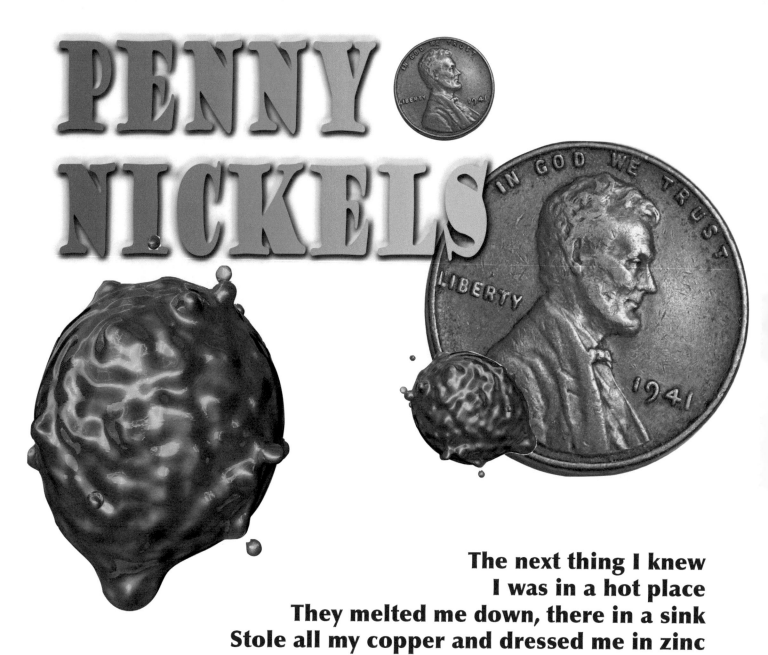

The next thing I knew
I was in a hot place
They melted me down, there in a sink
Stole all my copper and dressed me in zinc

A quick spray of copper so I would glow
They told me I was now ready to go
Back to the world where they had me sent
But I hate this life, living in "de basement"

PREACHER NOAH

Here's the message Noah preached
To ears that were dull and hearts that were hard
Perilous times now lay at hand
We need to repent, heed God's command
The earth's population had exploded in number
A beautiful place now evil-filled
Though the people were totally depraved
Noah kept preaching that they might be saved

They ate, they drank, they bought, they sold
Boastful, slanderous, ungrateful and proud
No one there cared about God
So, God quit sparing His rod
Noah finished building the ark
Now, ready to go, standing on top
He looked to the sky, then peered at the sod
Felt the first rain drops delivered by God.

GIRL OF THE FOUNTAIN

Bordered by mountains with a rampart view
At the edge of the world with time askew
Lies a hilltop fortress overlooking the sea
Reflecting a love that cannot be

We glimpse a girl flitting through
Alleys wrapped in folds of time
A fountain holds her memories
Memories, of a love sublime

A piece of song drifts across
The rippling water in a pool of green
Beyond the voices of her soul
Foreboding shadows can now be seen

Her heart beats a desperate rhythm
Gazing at the silhouette
Blended in this pool of love
Her eyes ablaze like the sun above

Alone in a love, meant for two
Frozen, all she does is stare
For between the silhouette and her soul
Memories of him are everywhere

FACES IN THE MIRROR

In a mirror by candlelight
Midst the nighttime air
I see a face with a silvery sheen
Very old, standing there

I see a face telling stories
Without a single word
Reality's mirror staring back
Memories now very blurred

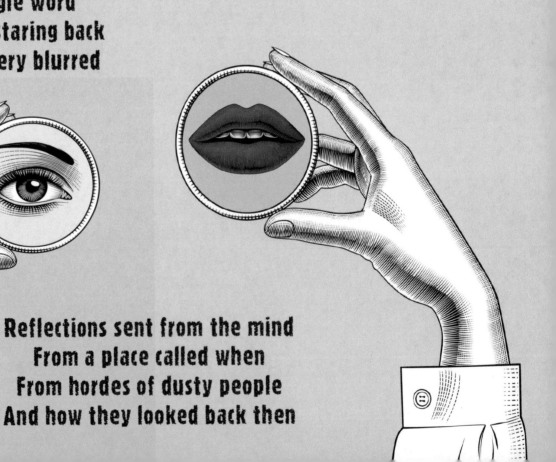

Reflections sent from the mind
From a place called when
From hordes of dusty people
And how they looked back then

FACES IN THE MIRROR

Remembering anything,
real or not
Reminding myself,
it's all I've got
I am the face who
came to stay
When all the others went
on their way

KING OF HOLLYWOOD

His expressions, his gestures
A smile that won't stop
A handsome, romantic charmer
A toy boy making his way to the top

In the Golden Years of Hollywood
With rich women paving his way
He's an avid pupil in their world
He moves in but he doesn't stay

Finally, a breakthrough from MGM
Clark Gable makes the big splash
His life is now a non-stop wonder
Immensely famous and loaded with cash

The King of Hollywood
was young
Just 59 when he
passed away
It was said he was
"Gone with the Wind"
Never again to see
a Hollywood day

FROM Sea to shining SEA

IN THE LAND THAT USED TO BE

We sing America the Beautiful
We see the amber waves of grain
We're dazzled by the purple mountains
We're told that selfish gain will stain
The gleaming alabaster cities
Now dimmed by human tears
They are the newest wilderness
That spiral through our fears
The pilgrims beat a thoroughfare
From sea to shining sea
Thus, fulfilling their patriot dream
While reaching for Thy jubilee
God did refine the gold
He shed His grace on thee
God, help us now to mend the flaws
In the land that used to be

PRAIRIE VIEWS

Boundless and beautiful
Under great curving skies
The swell of the prairie meets the horizon
Soul-melting scenery filling my eyes

Midst the ocean of solitude
Painted with colors and smells
Chirps and twitters crouch in the hollows
Prairie dog sentries are sounding their yells

Tumbleweeds kiss the grasses
Like feeble scratches on a blank page
Waves of gold, magnificent gold
Roll along into the sage

The dirt road stretches out
Unwinding into emptiness
Passing now a ramshackle shack
Built only yesterday, yesterday way back

Sounds of Del Rio radio waves
Soothes my country spirit
On this marvelous somber plain
Black smoke rises from a lonesome train

Luminous colors lay in the west
Shots of gold into dazzling silver
Trimmed with apricot and copper blend
The sun surrendering love to the end

Here we are blowing free
The Great Plains winds and little ole me
Singing His praises as we rejoice
The whistling prairie heard from my voice

RHYTHM AND BLUES

Strides with rhythmic chords
Srising from Buzzards Bay
Their echoes dancing on crested waves
like glitters of ashes on silvery graves
The tones are loud and long and deep
pulsing through my veins

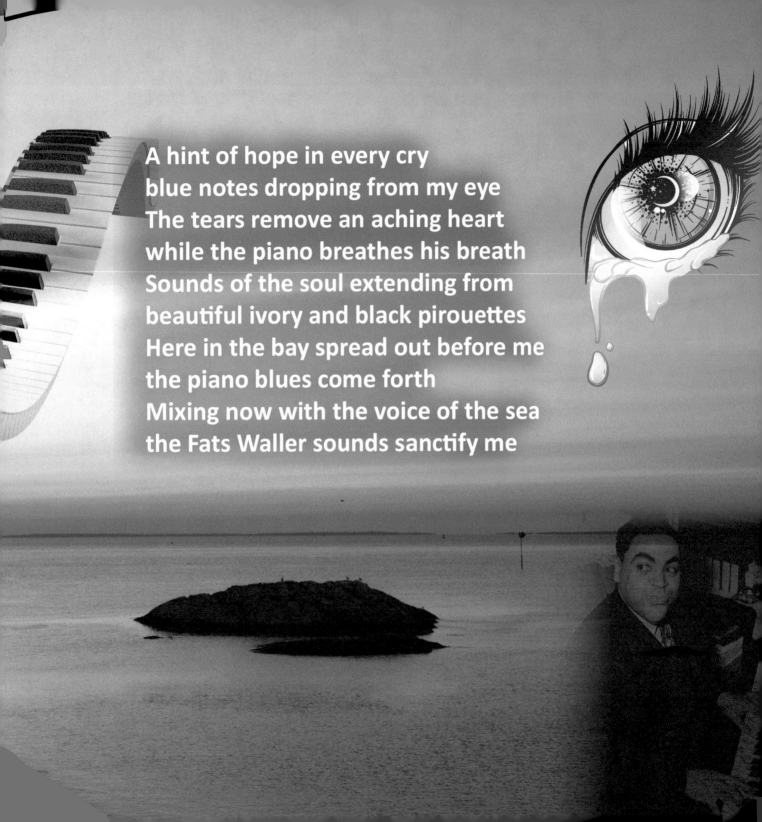

A hint of hope in every cry
blue notes dropping from my eye
The tears remove an aching heart
while the piano breathes his breath
Sounds of the soul extending from
beautiful ivory and black pirouettes
Here in the bay spread out before me
the piano blues come forth
Mixing now with the voice of the sea
the Fats Waller sounds sanctify me

CLEOPATRA

Sailing up the river Cydnus
On a barge with a gilded stern
Cleopatra is dressed as Venus
Irresistible, as we soon learn

Outspread sails of purple
Canapé of gold
Silver oars beating to music
Echoing flutes and harps, we are told

Beautiful young boys painted like cupids
Her maids like Sea Nymphs and Graces
Venus is here to feast now with Baachus
Amid a multitude of river-lined faces

The perfumes diffused themselves
From the vessel to the shore
Anxiously Antony awaits his guest
His life changing forever more

Antony is struck by her presence
The character that attended all that she did
He delights at the sound of her voice
He is bewitched and behaves like a kid

Antony, the great Roman ruler
Now squandering and fooling around
Cleopatra is the love of his life
Here on a new foreign ground

With stamps attached to their clothing
The post office delivered a trickle of tots
With "special handling" guidelines
Children were delivered; no, not in a box

"Freight Mail" was cheaper than a passenger ticket
So, the folks loaded them up
Into a boxcar with the bees and the bugs
And Sears Roebuck items, like blankets and rugs

HANDLED WITH CARE

These early 20th century touchstones
Accommodated families that were miles apart
The packages were never "lost in transit"
These special deliveries were made from the heart

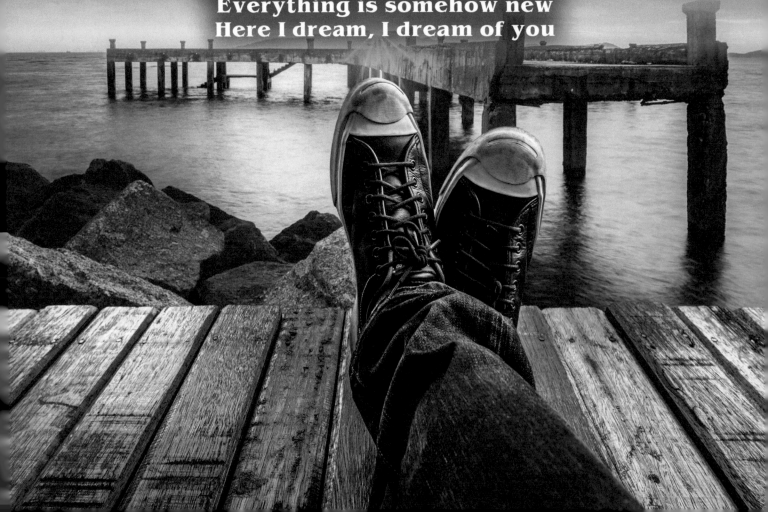

DREAMS OF YOU

Dwelling in my soul today
Beyond the power of mind or eye
From the sun the quivers fall
Quiet blending of earth and sky

In this kingdom by the sea
Midst the wonder of antiquity
Everything is somehow new
Here I dream, I dream of you

Strolling through the streets and squares
The smell of love is everywhere
The lapping sounds against the pier
I close my eyes and you are here

The solitude of paradise
Where the eye of heaven shines
Gleaming visions in waters blue
Here I dream, I dream of you

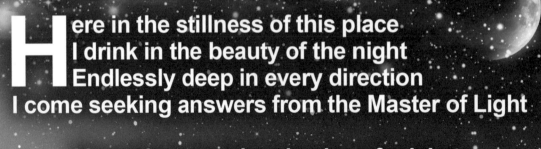

Here in the stillness of this place
I drink in the beauty of the night
Endlessly deep in every direction
I come seeking answers from the Master of Light

I hear the occasional voice of crickets
The hoot of the owl from up above
I watch the eyes of the skies winking
While waiting to hear the message of love

FEET OF CLAY

I lay claim unto this site
The presence of His eternal might
It holds answers for an impossible day
Answers for feet that are made out of clay

MESSAGE FROM AN EAGLE

Wearing my dark brown velvety coat
Beautifully groomed long white hair
I have my eyes on each one of you
As I speak to you from this chair

We have a republic if we can keep it
We need a group to watch for flaws
The abuses committed by elected officials
Just as the Supreme Court watches the laws

I heard George Washington say
Religion and morality were indispensable
Without religion, morals go
Without morals, virtues go
Without virtues, we cannot see
The principles of Freedom and Liberty

An imperfect, emotional man
Reaches for stardust with his right hand
Sequined shirts; shimmying time
Writing words in Longfellow rhyme

DIAMONDS
are Forever

A Tribute to Neil Diamond

The love of the crowd caresses his skin
The reward of applause he is destined to win
Then wrapping the world with infectious sound
He watches the stardust fall to the ground

HORSES

Before she was a school girl
Before she learned to read
There was a love for horses
To fill a gap, to fill a need
Today that need remains
Felt in the heart, carried through reins
Stares from deep-set almond eyes

Yearning for love under now autumn skies
Horse people need only a horse
Their DNA is different
A perfect escape from the mundane
At the end of the day only whispers remain
With hair streaming out behind her
And the power of the beast beneath
The sun and wind have their role
But the four feet below is what moves her soul

SHACK BY THE SEA

Here am I, a seaside shack
Anchored in a peaceful lagoon
In a quiet place at the edge of the world
Watching the glimmers of waters pearled

The sweeping patterns of today
Push all memories far away
New scents are washing to the shore
The golden voice is heard no more

Oh sea, oh sea, majestic sea
The love I witnessed in my lair
Feeling every throbbing moment
The breezes touching golden hair

Though this vision belongs to me
Through broken windows, I can see
A treasure of life from long ago
Ebbing now in a golden glow

Then suddenly rising from your frothy wave
I hear voices from your watery grave
Melodies tucked into breezes so near
Wrapping my frame as the sky sheds its tear

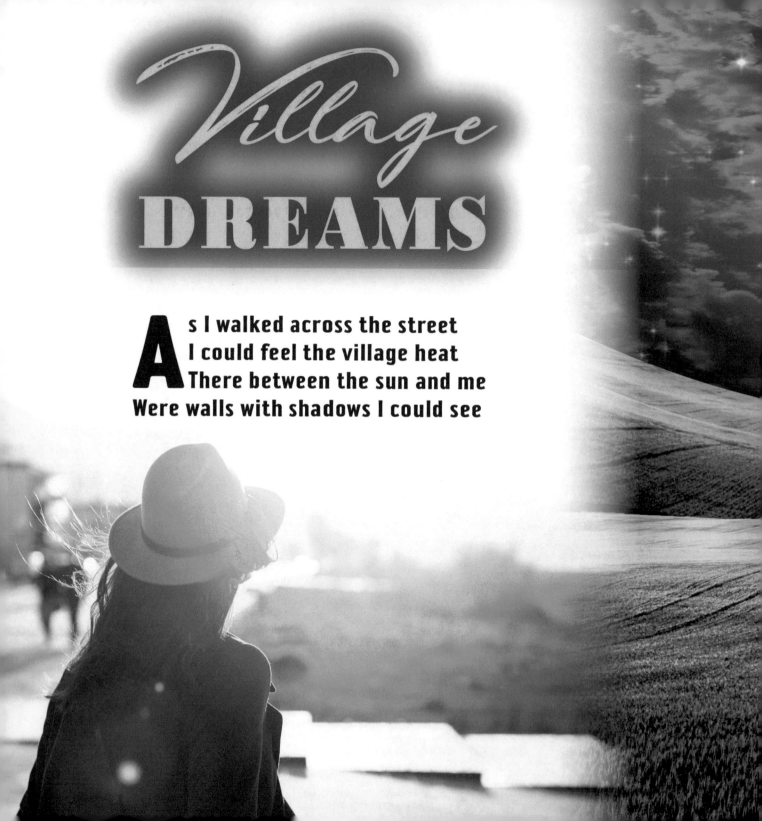

Village DREAMS

As I walked across the street
I could feel the village heat
There between the sun and me
Were walls with shadows I could see

Hazy sequences from memory lane
Shimmers from the past
There beneath the mellowing sun
The wandering shadows had just begun

I walked the village within that dream
Finding words, I never thought to speak
I found that room where past lives live
I found those thoughts that were mine to give

Here in a village that rose from the plains
From a street that feels your blood in its veins
I found meadows blossomed with stars
Words for the moment, now, this song is ours!

Singing a song like no other
Truly a cappella style
The unusual strains of a bass
Crossing the ocean mile after mile

This magnificent creature of the deep
Sings an unrequited love song
Performed in a frequency that no others use
A song from this whale now rings loud and long

We may call him a Blue 52
For the Hertz he sings cannot be heard
Crying for companionship that never comes
Those beautiful females hear not a word!

Hand of God

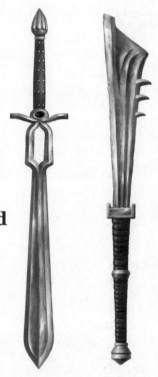

City after city, they moved along
    Charging horsemen with gleaming spears
    Led by Sennacherib, the Assyrian king
To see what chaos they might bring

Five thousand princes in gold chariots
Eighty thousand knights in shining armor
Eighty-five thousand swordsmen, the butchering kind
Surrounding Jerusalem with evil in mind

A blasphemous letter to King Hezekiah
"You think you can withstand my hand?
You are now a part of my lair
Just like those peoples, of Ashur, out there"

Holding words that ridiculed God
King Hezekiah rent his clothes
Shrieked with grief and despair
Ordered his people to kneel down in prayer

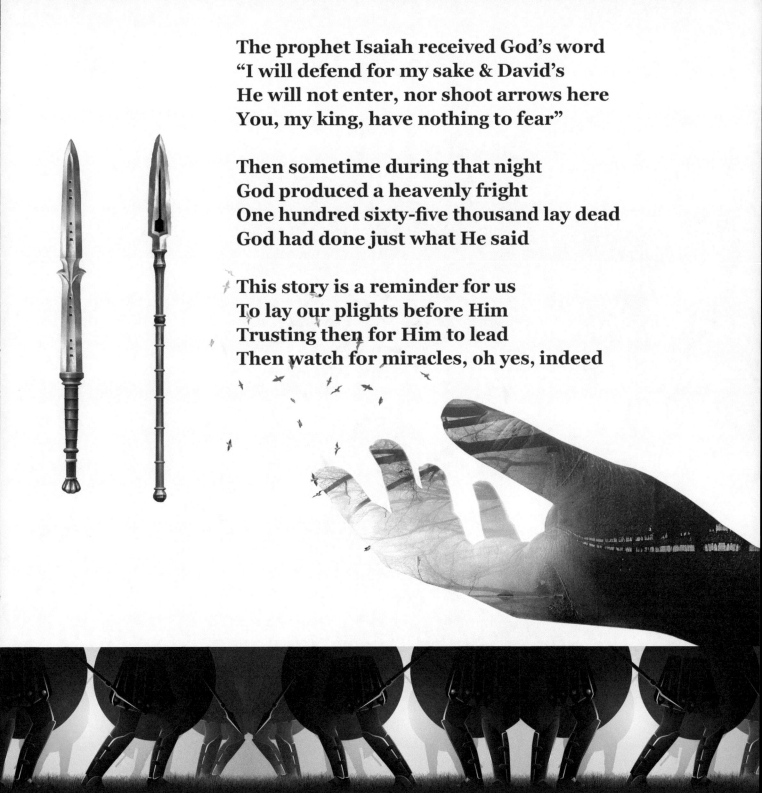

The prophet Isaiah received God's word
"I will defend for my sake & David's
He will not enter, nor shoot arrows here
You, my king, have nothing to fear"

Then sometime during that night
God produced a heavenly fright
One hundred sixty-five thousand lay dead
God had done just what He said

This story is a reminder for us
To lay our plights before Him
Trusting then for Him to lead
Then watch for miracles, oh yes, indeed

Most of us do not know
What our founding fathers said
About the newly found government
Creating the words as they were led

The name American belongs to you
We walk upon untrodden ground
May the Father of mercy scatter light
On this path that we have found

No morn ever dawned more favorable
During those years passed through dimly
We shall not depart from this road
Which Providence has pointed us to, so plainly

Liberty, once lost, is lost forever
Democracy never lasts long
It wastes, exhausts, murders itself
Wholly inadequate becomes the new song

FOUNDING FATHERS

What little my countrymen know
What precious blessings they're in possession of
No other people on earth enjoy
This wonderful land splashed with God's love

When I reflect, that God is just
Indeed, I tremble for my country
Can we be ignorant and free?
That never was and never will be

STORMY DREAMS

A cold wind is blowing from the north
Hovering downward in uncertain flight
Stormy dreams are dimming the sight
As snow flurries blur the day into night

In this diamond-dusted wilderness
With memories of another place
A sense of longing is standing there
Tonight, catching her unaware

He is a stranger
Wandering through
Burning footprints in the snow
Why he stopped, we do not know

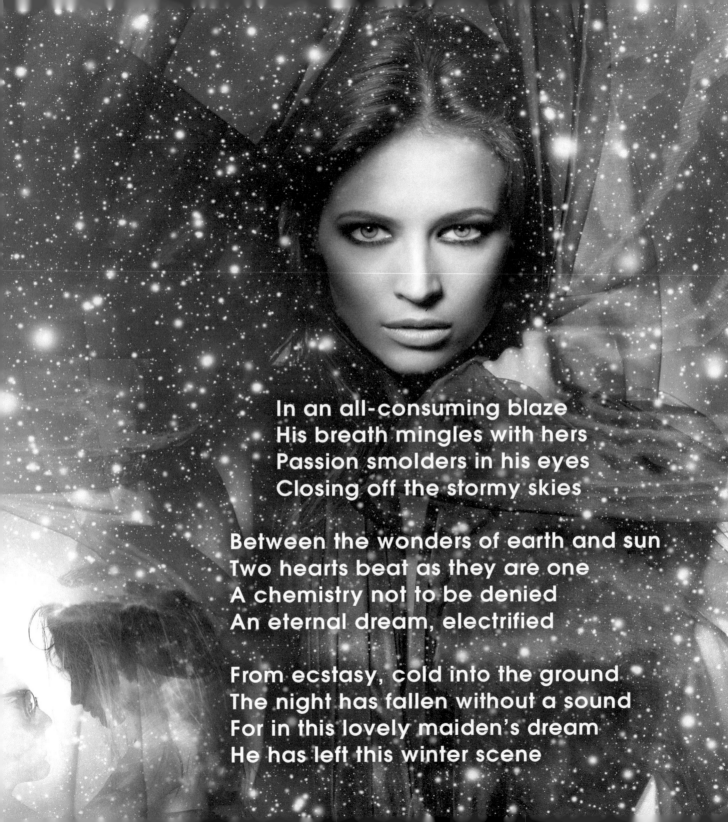

In an all-consuming blaze
His breath mingles with hers
Passion smolders in his eyes
Closing off the stormy skies

Between the wonders of earth and sun
Two hearts beat as they are one
A chemistry not to be denied
An eternal dream, electrified

From ecstasy, cold into the ground
The night has fallen without a sound
For in this lovely maiden's dream
He has left this winter scene

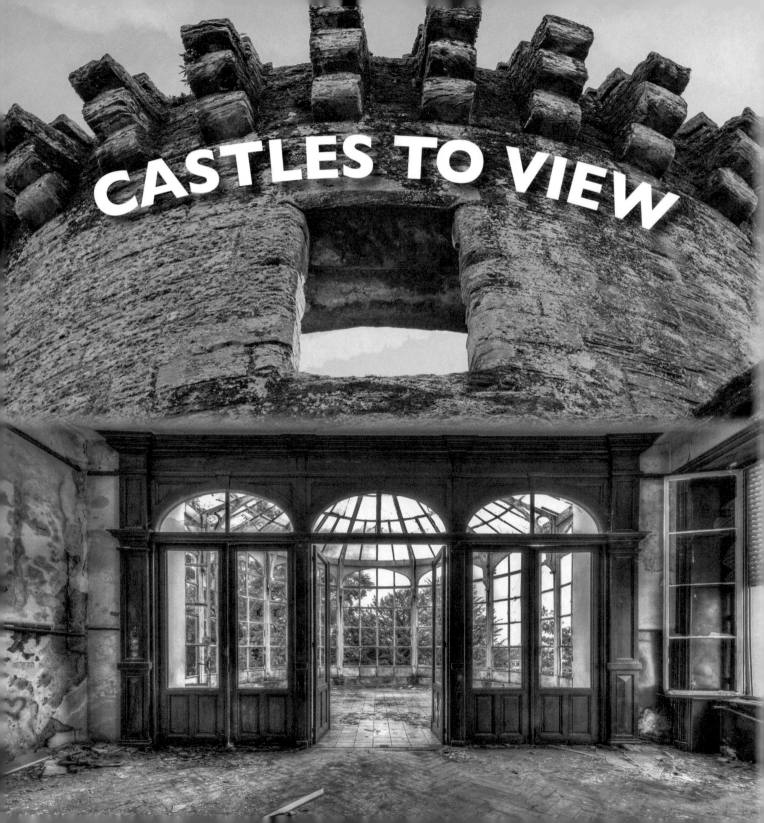

CASTLES TO VIEW

Under the grime of centuries
Hidden in forgotten times
There remain the towers
Layers of stones in many designs

Scars of survival and victory
Echoes of pomp and ceremony
Celebrations in the Great Hall
Secure behind the thick 'curtain wall'

Little by little the old world crumbled
Blurring the differences between then and now
Castles and strongholds remain to be seen
Above the white cliffs and out on the green

Dank walls rise between towers
Moss-and ivy-covered today
In the dungeons hidden below
Lays a dangerous twisted passageway

Recalling to memory a feudal lord
Vassals and peasants in a frenzied world
Life in the castle would not be my choice
But history holds a much different voice

MOONLIGHT

The May moonlight is hanging low
Unlocking memories from years ago
A slice of time from beyond the gate
A story of love that could not wait

The night is damp and cool
The hollows on the terrace are shimmering pools
The space is filled with dragonflies
A lamplight reflects the light of her eyes

MEMORIES

Our first walk, our first touch
Lingering now as a fantasy
In every star, in every breeze
In every leaf that falls from the trees

Holding a lily in her hand
Beneath the woody vine
Witnessed by the old-stone gnome
Her world blended then with mine

Today, in this magical place
I see her hair as she stood there
A meeting that took place by chance
Leaving my memory to live in a trance

She was the enforcer
Stoic and strong
Funny and fierce
Her whole life long
Led by the dreams of her heart
Living each moment as a gifted pearl

Pearls for Barbara

Savoring the journey with great love in her life

A president's mother, a president's wife

Her soul has done what it came to do

Leaving uncountable treasures

Immortal now is she

In that place where we long to be

The air around us has grown still

That living love is now living above

Pearls have slipped from a string

A cascade of pearls that she did bring

ACROBATS

From out of history's mist
come murals and carvings in stones
unforgettable, rich flavored records
given by humans that God alone owns

Thrills of ancient acrobatics
backflips in the air
agile bodies, twisting, bending
Records there for us to share

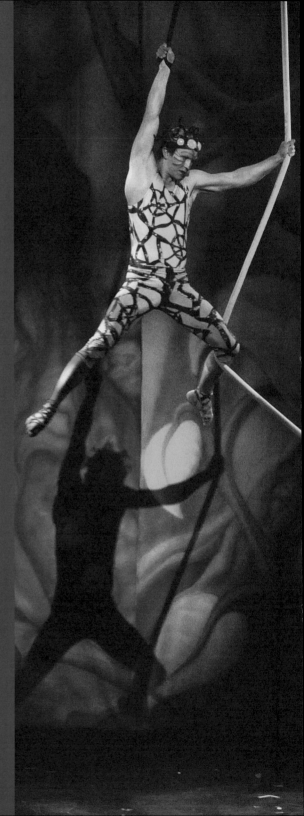

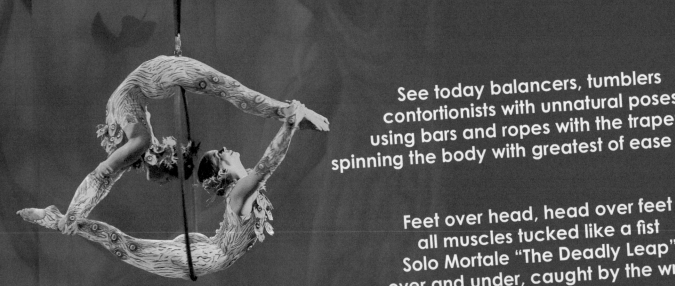

See today balancers, tumblers
contortionists with unnatural poses
using bars and ropes with the trapeze
spinning the body with greatest of ease

Feet over head, head over feet
all muscles tucked like a fist
Solo Mortale "The Deadly Leap"
over and under, caught by the wrist

There was Alfredo Cordona
whose talent we cannot conceive
Triple somersaults were mastered
at speeds hard to believe

How shall we honor
the kings and queens of the air?
in thinking about Jules Leotard
we could go out and buy us a pair

Reflections standing
Amongst captured moments
Leaving marks upon her soul
Silver filaments wet with rain
Time and tears taking their toll

MARKS

She feels his breath
His pulse beats deep
In these dark hours, she cannot sleep
She walks the road
Searches the sky
All the while, wondering why

Day after day, night after night
Reciting her story of scars
Yearning for something new on the pages
She looks up to see a blanket of stars

OF MAN

Then some wisdom comes to mind
The stars are scarred, but they still shine

White Sands World

Another world, glistening white
Ever changing but always the same
Remains of an old sea floor
Blown out of heaven's door

Laying in southern New Mexico
The winds blow the sand-like snow
Very brittle and fragile crystals
Ever changing the sandy ripples

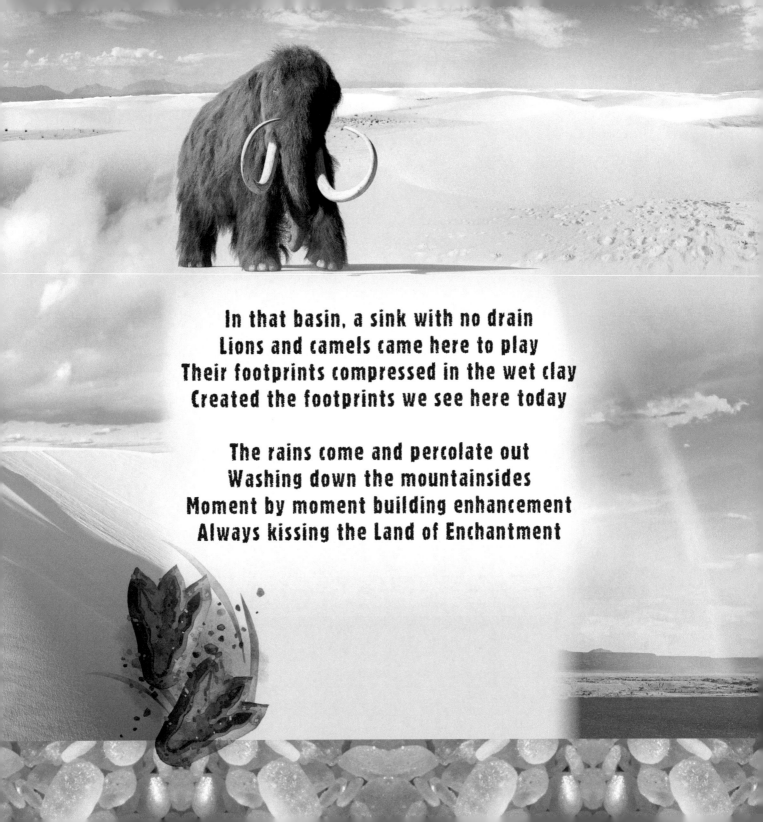

In that basin, a sink with no drain
Lions and camels came here to play
Their footprints compressed in the wet clay
Created the footprints we see here today

The rains come and percolate out
Washing down the mountainsides
Moment by moment building enhancement
Always kissing the Land of Enchantment

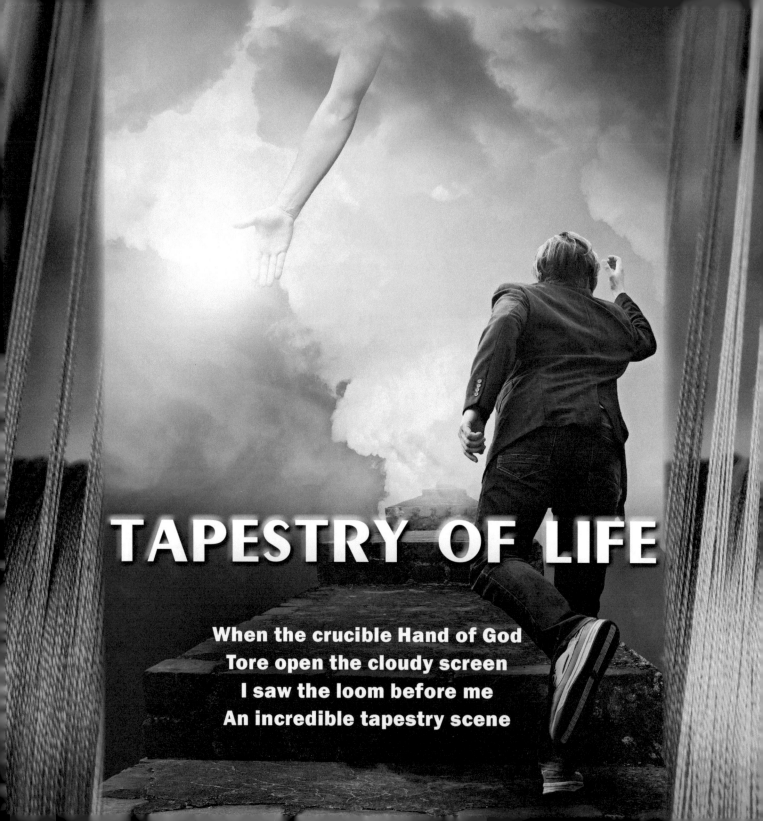

TAPESTRY OF LIFE

When the crucible Hand of God
Tore open the cloudy screen
I saw the loom before me
An incredible tapestry scene

Threads designing the patterns of life
Pillars of memories woven through
Creating a picture that forever will live
From threads of free will of all that we do
Forging one's own destiny
With weavings of passion and pain

Unraveled threads were touched and re-stitched
Forgiveness and promise removing life's stain
This is when some threads I see
Ones that affect my destiny
Silken threads tucked in a fold
Silken threads made of gold

HOPE TO HORROR

On the Pacific side of the Andes Mountains
Amid tropical trees pushing for light
Beyond the end of civilized roads
The warring savages lay out of sight

Believing the gospel preached
Five young men answer the call
Their hearts equipped with flames of fire
Hoping the tribe will welcome them all

Months of caressing with giving of gifts
There appears to be a welcome exchange
Believing that this was the day
They landed the piper on the sands of the bay

The Huaorani people received a false message
Delivered by evil alive in their midst
Screamed out of the forest with nine-foot spears
The five do die; so young in their years

Their footprints remain on that stretch of sand
Forgiven tribesmen with new willing hearts
Their voices reverberating throughout the years
Now walk with God on a trail drenched with tears

Lost in the sounds of time
through the blue smoke, rhythms and rhyme
Mingling with the stars up above
Binding sounds, chords that we love

Classical ribbons creating hues
like an angel kissing the strings
Samba rhythms born in Brazil
Epitomes of words that are with us still

LATIN

LOVE

Magical music painted on silence
Inexpressible voices of silk
Two gods blending in harmony
unwrapping love for the world to see

Through quiet nights of the universe
the Latin love springs forth
Quiet nights, like when we dream
is sung by Sinatra and Antonio Jobim

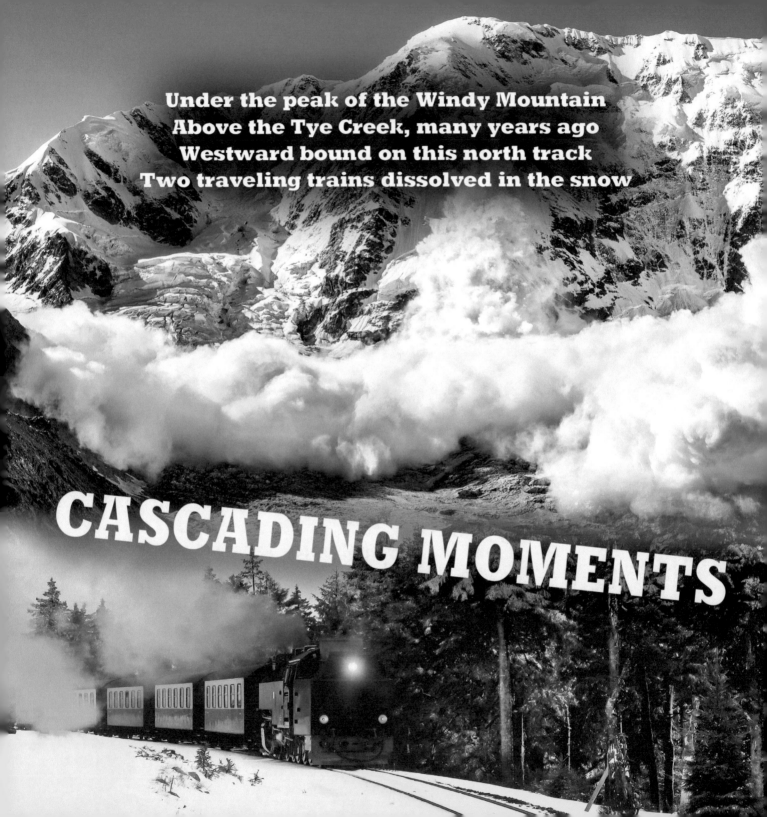

Under the peak of the Windy Mountain
Above the Tye Creek, many years ago
Westward bound on this north track
Two traveling trains dissolved in the snow

CASCADING MOMENTS

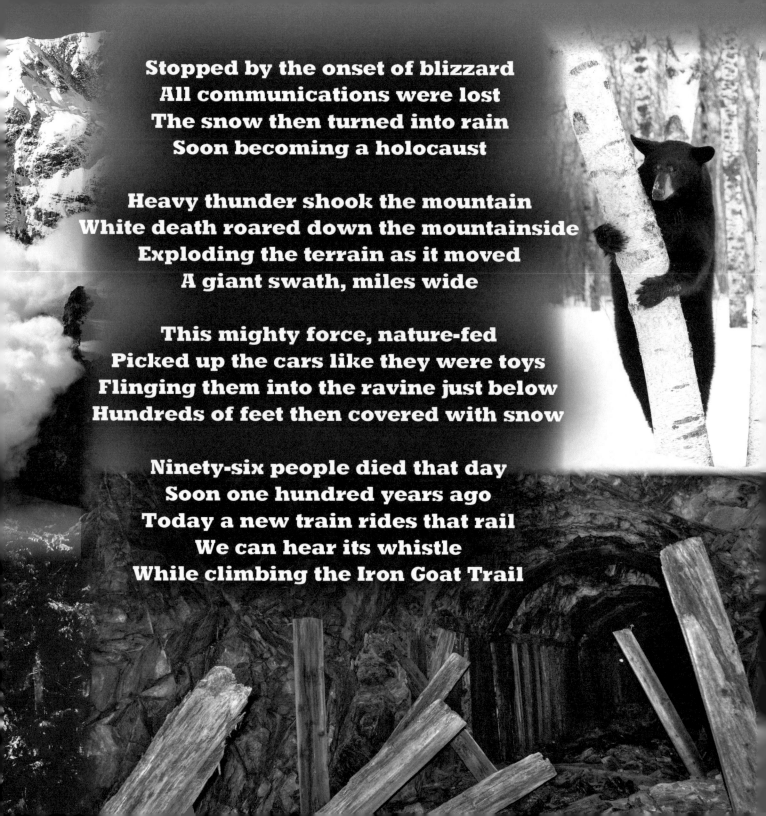

Stopped by the onset of blizzard
All communications were lost
The snow then turned into rain
Soon becoming a holocaust

Heavy thunder shook the mountain
White death roared down the mountainside
Exploding the terrain as it moved
A giant swath, miles wide

This mighty force, nature-fed
Picked up the cars like they were toys
Flinging them into the ravine just below
Hundreds of feet then covered with snow

Ninety-six people died that day
Soon one hundred years ago
Today a new train rides that rail
We can hear its whistle
While climbing the Iron Goat Trail

David's Dance

In the City of David
The crowds gathered this day
Waiting for the Ark of the Covenant
After many long years of being away

God enthroned between two cherubim
Was being delivered today
Into the Promised Kingdom
Where David waited in the archway

Hearing the sounds of reedy winds
David stripped off his kingly attire
To a robe of fine linen, an ephod
Humbly, to receive, this gift from God

Now following this precious gift
Amid castanets, cymbals and lyre
King David begins to dance
Whirling and leaping, his heart on fire

Loaves of cakes were given to all
A celebration of God who had chosen him
Creator and created, merging as one
One more step, towards the birth of His Son

Clark Kent

*L*ooking at life in arrears
It's not always as it appears
Surprises come along the way
Judgment, not for me to say

In the Bavarian Mountains
Death came visiting today
No one there was surprised
That a woman named Brigitte had passed away

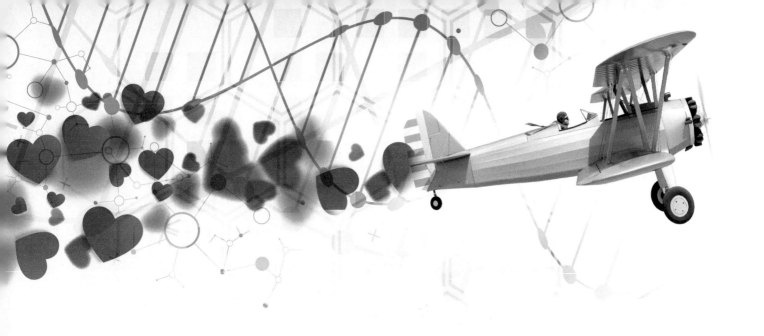

When her children go through things
There, hidden for no one to see
One hundred-fifty love letters
All signed by *Mr. C.*

They recognized the letters
As being from their dad
That charming but mysterious man
The greatest love their mom ever had

The children were always told
Their father would not return
If they spoke of him too much
Even she had a lot to learn

When this story was unwrapped
They found cousins living close
They too knew this Clark Kent
A very nice man who paid their rent

As discoveries unfolded
With DNA testing off by zero
Confirming for the world to see
Mr. Superman, an international hero

That handsome young airplane pilot
Who crossed the Atlantic in one day
In his "Spirit of St. Louis" aircraft
Charles Lindbergh had feet of clay

The
Danube Blue

As I awoke this morning
Cuddling the soft European linens
My dream of a lifetime had come true
I was cruising down the Danube Blue

Tasting the finest vintage wines
Chocolate muffins and madeleines
Exploring every port of call
Not just one, I had them all!

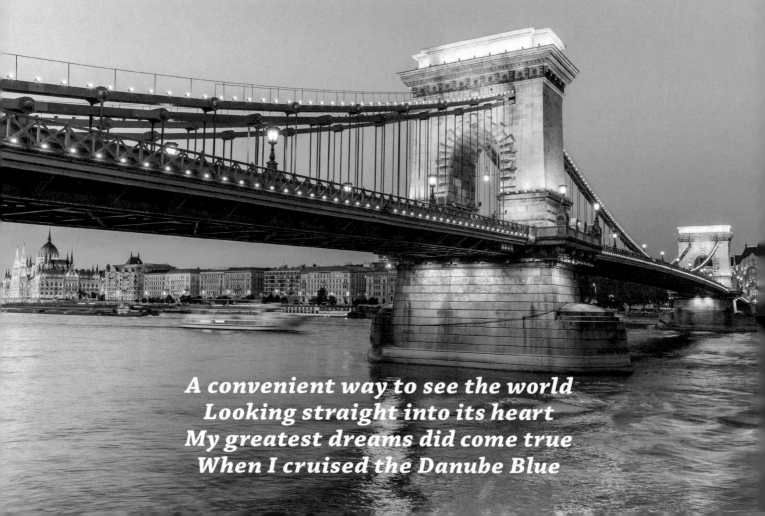

Storybook castles lit up the sky
As the ship went meandering by
Magnificent vistas I wandered through
While sailing down this Danube Blue

Renaissance and Rococo designs
Jewels I found along the way
Doorways to culture and customs
Relaxed my vibes at the end of each day

A convenient way to see the world
Looking straight into its heart
My greatest dreams did come true
When I cruised the Danube Blue

THROUGH
DREAMS

A new chapter in life is about to be written
Speaking the language of your soul
Words to twirl around your space
An impossible, improbable, inevitable goal

Answers yet to be discovered
Hidden dreams to be revealed
Goals unreached but aims to strive
With a leap of faith becomes alive
When dreams come true
Your world is made new
You may fly and touch the sky
Only God knows what you may do
You are never given a dream
Without the power to make it come true
A new chapter in life can be written
Follow your dreams, it's up to you

On this side of heaven
Where the spirit flows
Where hopes and dreams come true
North of beautiful where we walked
Touching the vanishing silvery dew
Deep, deep, silence surrounded the shore
Breezes caressed the craggy moor
We blew kisses into the wind
We saw the beauty of dreams unpinned

The Kiss

Ah, the wonder of that place
To have seen the joy written on your face
In dreams, boundaries do not exist
I know it was real, for I was kissed

The Mimosa, a dilapidated clipper
Lay in Liverpool dock
Readying herself for a memorable voyage
Patagonia bound, sixty days by the clock

Seven thousand miles to carry the Welsh
Emigrants filled with hopes and dreams
To a land where Welshmen can be their own king
And God be praised, correctly it seems

Wales Beyond Wales

Three non-conforming preachers
Leading a group of one-fifty-three
Singles and married with children
With sails unfurled, headed for sea
One hundred and fifty years have now passed
The Welsh settlements still remain
Patagonia got a new little Wales
Thanks to the Mimosa and the strength of her sails

The tree is tall
Its branches long
It wears a gentle swaying crown
Giving waves of melody
Leaves then dance on their way down

TREES
TO

Listen closely
You'll hear its song
From beyond the bark and knots
That melodious drifting sound
Conveying love; as it talks

I need you to be a tree
To stand as tall as you can be
To grow your roots deep inside
Be my shade with all your pride

I want to feel your leaves fall
Amber, gold; I'll love them all
And when rough winds head our way
Cuddle you close on that blustery day!

LOVE

CANYONS OF THE WORLD

A path to places not found on a map
Crooked, winding, thorny and steep
Murky nights, loathsome days
The beating of wings in the canyons so deep

Below that hawk, circling above
Whose eyes were on me right from the start
Swooping down with talons so sharp
Talons that sunk deep in my heart

Today between the misty clouds
While reaching for an amazing view
I pray to heal the scars of my heart
Knowing the hawk needs healing too

Just as the sun was rising
The first of the shots were fired
Now pursuing freedom
The Minutemen were inspired

The express riders delivered messages
Together with bells, bonfires, trumpets and drum
Sending word from town to town
Alerting all should the Redcoats come

LET FREEDOM RING

The country people lit their beacons
Beyond the swamps and slips of the sea
Say'n "Give 'em the guts of our guns
If'n this war has to be"

From Lexington to Concord
Chasing Redcoats down the lane
Under the trees at the turn of the road
Pausing only to fire and reload

On this April day in 1775
The farmers did not know
That yet an unfurled flag would fly
Today was merely do or die!

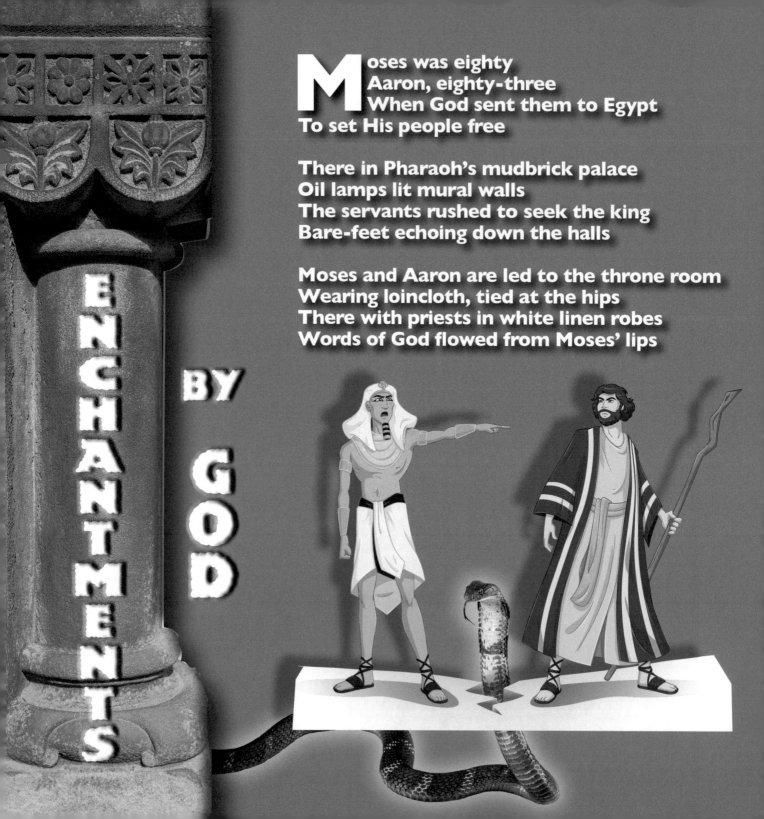

ENCHANTMENTS

BY GOD

Moses was eighty
Aaron, eighty-three
When God sent them to Egypt
To set His people free

There in Pharaoh's mudbrick palace
Oil lamps lit mural walls
The servants rushed to seek the king
Bare-feet echoing down the halls

Moses and Aaron are led to the throne room
Wearing loincloth, tied at the hips
There with priests in white linen robes
Words of God flowed from Moses' lips

"Prove yourself" Pharaoh said
With a hardened heart
So, Aaron threw down his stake
Which quickly turned into a cobra snake

The priests were Jannes & Jambres
Skilled Egyptian magicians
They pulled out staffs from inside their robes
Hoping to change the Godly conditions

By pressing the nape of a snake's neck
These wise men created a catalepsy
Now stiff and straight as a rod
They flung them down to challenge this God

But the rod of Aaron and Moses
Consumed the rods of these priests
Showing the superiority of Yahweh
Confounding their senses on this very first day!

Original art, mysteriously deep
Cosmic fires, nourishing flames
There in its center blended in swirls
Is a wave of an ocean and a hand, holding pearls

Painted feelings on a canvas of love
A precious gift now more than a dream

Girl
of His
Dream

A Tribute to
Roy Orbison

Something beautiful, sent from above
A handful of pearls for the girl that he loves

Red hot colors, artfully arranged
Inspired by the voice from the bay
Dipping the brush in a silvery hue
Hearing the words, "I found them for you"

Empty vessels, breathing lies
Laying in ashes where souls can rise
Born from stories we tell ourselves
I know without me, my fear dies

hope & faith
overcom
fear

This is a journey from the inside
Where scary feelings turn into hope
When all of what you fear to do
Shines very bright when it shines from you

Why waste the life that you have been given?
The treasure you seek lies in your fire
Forgive and forget the fearful past
Grab on to hope for it will last

Wisdom will guide you through your space
For wisdom is issued by divine grace
In the midst of love, we need not fear
For the light that shines will always be near

face
your
fears

Freedom for the New Land

Seventeen days in June
With prowess and polish of pen
In the red-brick home of Jacob Graff
Our America was about to begin

He had a single-eye to reason
Declaring facts that did exist
Penned in the language of truth
Rights, not favors, he did insist

Foremost son of American enlightenment
Thomas Jefferson did step forth
Laying out power, jurisdiction and right
A document flowing in freedom's new light

The Declaration of Independence
A revolutionary statement
Pledging lives, fortunes and honor in deed
His words becoming America's new creed

Into the glowing light
I am swept like a wingless bird
Amid the city of purest white
With pillars rising into the light

An orchestra of voices
Sounds throughout the halls
Welcomes me to this place
Enchanting echoes of heavenly calls

Shimmering with crystals
This enormous building stands
Holding wisdom from the ages
On papyrus, clay and leather pages

HEAVENLY LIBRARY

As far as my eye can see
Row upon row, shelf upon shelf
Documents waiting to be read
Even a scroll about myself

Everything ever written or said
Was in this vast domain
Every thought that I now held
Could not remain the same

This library, high in the heavens
Holds records of the infinite spirit
While we on earth walk on our way
Adding to records, day by day

Goodrich Ghosts

North of the village of Goodrich
Standing high above the River Wye
The ghosts of two lovers glide
Under the cover, the dark of the sky
Step into medieval history
Beneath a full moon of its past
Taste the tea, nibble the cakes
Feel the lingering tingle from the moves that she makes
Warmed by wine and the fireplace
The two lovers meet to discuss their escape
Away from the constant bombardment
Hoping for a new life that they could make

They mounted a slick blackened steed
Made their escape through the kissing gate
Headed through the rocky spur
Anxiously proceeding an unknown fate
Heavy rains had swollen the river
The horse lost his footing, the couple clung on
Through the raging waters, embracing
Finally, death, the two were then gone
Today at Goodrich Castle
Nestled below the leafy hill
Into the night, two specters stare
From the ramparts and their ruinous lair

LOVE AFFAIR

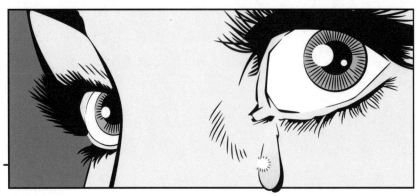

I n a yacht, moored at the dock
Cold, cold moments, were happening there
Dead emotions, stretched and skewed
The ash remains of a love affair

A sideways glance, a heavy look
Looks that grazed her heart
She stared back in numbing silence
Feeling distant and apart

Unpleasant and disturbing
Exchanging blinding words

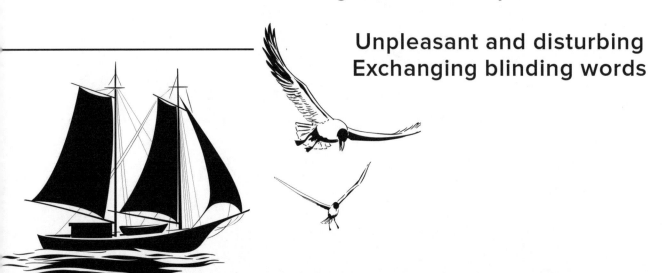

Joining then Cupid's chain
Eyes of regret, enduring pain

Stooping down to hear dead voices
Whispers of that long-gone day
When a love affair is over
Is there something more to say?

Oh, the vastness of this word
Paints a giant picture blue
Covering most of our own earth
Influences climate and weather too

It has a luminescence
Which extends for miles at night
First noticed by ancient sailors
Now captured by satellite

To a depth near seven miles
In Guam's Mariana Trench
We find on oceans lowest level
Hydrothermal vents

Like chimneys
Rising from the ocean's floor
Spewing clouds of thick black smoke
A soup, from nature's oven door

OCEANS

Totally separate from the world of light
Giant tube worms eight feet tall
Feeding millions of shrimp and crab
An ecosystem, the ocean's mall

HARVEST

In the springtime, the seed is laid
The sun shines on the rain
Until the green on soil is seen
Covering the field's terrain

Then, as time moves along
The plants stretch out from their ground
Plants lifting their proud heads
Ripe in season, wearing a crown

TIME

The time for harvest then arrives
A time to reap the harvest gold
To reap that beautiful planting
To watch a beautiful field unfold

I am standing where autumn winds blow
Prepping for the winter snow
Harvesting every field I see
Following a force stronger than me

ORIGINAL BOND

Greatest spy in history
A Ukrainian Jew by birth
A spy of extraordinary skill
Traveling to the ends of the earth

A Rosenblum named Shlomo
Revolutionized the espionage game
He joined the British intelligence
After selecting a new Irish name

Fluent in seven languages
Held a motto to trust no one
A master of deception
Uses impersonates while in the bastion

Living as Sidney George Reilly
He loved fast women and the high-life he spawned
Until his murder in Russia
He was the original, Bond, James Bond

Majestic Messages

Twinkling stars in the ethereal blue
A signal in the skies
Holy voices, melodious sounds
Resounds in their ears and visionary eyes
Mounting the desert camels
The Persian wise men did go
Carrying with them the treasures
 Isaiah's instructions from so long ago
Frankincense and myrrh from the forest
Gold from the local mine

Balthazar, Melchior and Gaspar
The birth of a ruler they set out to find
Passing through the space of Herod
Their story they gleefully shared
Herod jealously wanted to know more
To murder this child, because he was scared
The beautiful Magi delivered their gifts
To the Maker, the Monarch, the Savior of all
Hearing advice from a dream from above
Took another route home
To save a Savior they love

Someone lives within
One not there from the start
The only one who knew the words
Of the music from my heart
That is when life began
God intended you be seen
With a glade and serenade
Moonbeams bringing me my dream
You are the reason I feel warm

Song of the HEART

You are the reason for my smile
You are what money cannot buy
You are a gift come from the sky
Here is my toast to you
To all I dream, real and true
To all the time, old and gray
To many years of yesterday

WINGS

In the fog of early dawn
On this cold sunless shore
Silent and invisible, I wait
Illusions are deep
I cannot sleep

I cannot see the horizon
The scene is dank and gray
I wait for the sun to paint new views
The surf is curled
I wait for the world

As the sun peeks over the bridge
Unfolding a pallet of color
I hear the Voice from within saying
Rise up and fly
Into the sky

Then I feel the winds of the Spirit
Lift me to my dreams
Feel the tugging of my wings
Now my spirit flies
And so, do I!

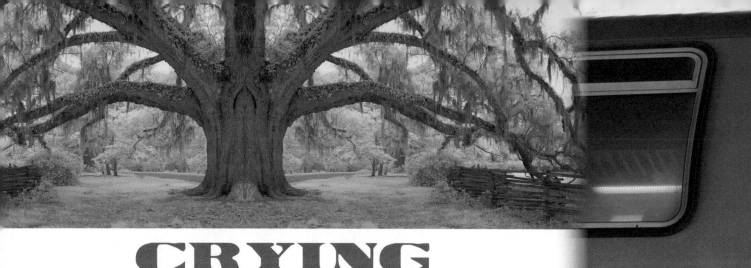

CRYING EAGLE

It was a day in November 1910
When one by one to the station they went
An Abram
A Nelson
A Henry
A Paul
A Frank
A Ben
And a Charles, that's all!

The seven boarded a deluxe sleeper car
For a two-day trip down the coast
Wearing disguises and using fake names
This meeting of minds still haunts like a ghost

Six plutocrats, all self-selected
By Senator Nelson Aldrich
To create a new system in light of banks crashing
A ruse of "duck hunting" was used for the masking

Among the six, we find Daddy Warbucks
Paul Warburg was his real name
His family was bankers-Rothschild-connected
With urging from Aldrich to America came

By train they concluded their journey
Aldrich, Warburg and five cronies
To a town called Brunswick, then on by ferry
To an island called Jekyll where all seven did tarry

Amid gnarly oaks and Spanish moss
The financial gurus pleased their powers
Within ten days they created a plan
Then the Federal Reserve Banking began

One hundred years later we see in reflecting
Just how this method of banking has been
The Rothschilds, Warburgs, Rockefellers and Morgans
Have all increased their assets
But we who labor, day onto day
Are left with inflation, high taxes and fears
A national debt and an eagle with tears!

Your Destiny

Come to someplace real
Come to someplace you can feel
Somewhere you have never been
Created by ink and sharp-point pen

Invite yourself to come inside
To where that beautiful light is lit
Join the thought of cherished dreams
Weave airy threads from where you sit

From the places where you have walked
Possible futures lie in the wait
Wanting to break through your walls
Walk you through the gilded gate

Attach yourself to your dream
Back it with consuming fire
Live with intentions of God almighty
Let passions become a burning desire

Make it big, make it grand
Close your eyes, commit your plan
You are creating your destiny
Most spectacular place on earth to see

FAKE NEWS!

Since the birth of the printing press
When all the bread-crumbs were laid
Humans have had a spinning machine
A creative place where words get paid

A journalist writing with honor and pride
Has a pedigree which we can see
But distorted images did arise
Self-scripted fiction, loaded with lies

Bogus stories created by trolls
Putting it out there, oh how it stinks
Truth reverberating with the lies
Absorbed by readers whose fears find the links

Today we have Buzzfeed, click-bait and others
Even a mis-trusted mainstream media
Creating shoddy error-filled news
Presented by writers with hate that he spews

Fiction and fabrications
Between the truth and lies
Today I choose the sounds of silence
Laying down the screaming whys

CHICAGO HEAT

Arm-in-arm with two gals that he knows
This dapper young man to the movie goes
Wearing gray striped trousers
With white canvas shoes
Destined to be tomorrow's big news

"Manhattan Melodrama" starring Clark Gable
A cool, cool movie for this heat-drenched night
At that theatre on the north-side of town
He dips into a seat, makes not a sound

James Lawrence, or so he was called
Accompanied tonight by a 'woman in red'
Exits the theatre at 10:30 pm
Not even a thought that he soon would be dead

There is a man standing near
Out on the sidewalk when he does appear
The two exchange piercing eyes
Before a volley of bullets issues demise

At the entrance to a now-famous alley
You can see chalk lines on the concrete
Even reports of a ghostly blur
While remembering the short life of John Dillinger

CORRUPTION

Hear my baneful ideology
As I step forth today
Knowing when you look at me
I'm not really what you see

Refining my voice as suits the times
My words are wrapped in a shroud of deceit
Seducing the hungry, hopeless and broken
Enjoying a good life, embracing the elite

Clothed in the finest linen, I stand
Amid the green glow of political corruption
Reaching out with a slimy hand
Controlling the world from the swampland

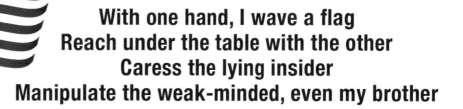

With one hand, I wave a flag
Reach under the table with the other
Caress the lying insider
Manipulate the weak-minded, even my brother

I am corruption
Stepping out from my lair
Come, just a little closer
Sniff my smelly underwear......

FROZEN IN TIME

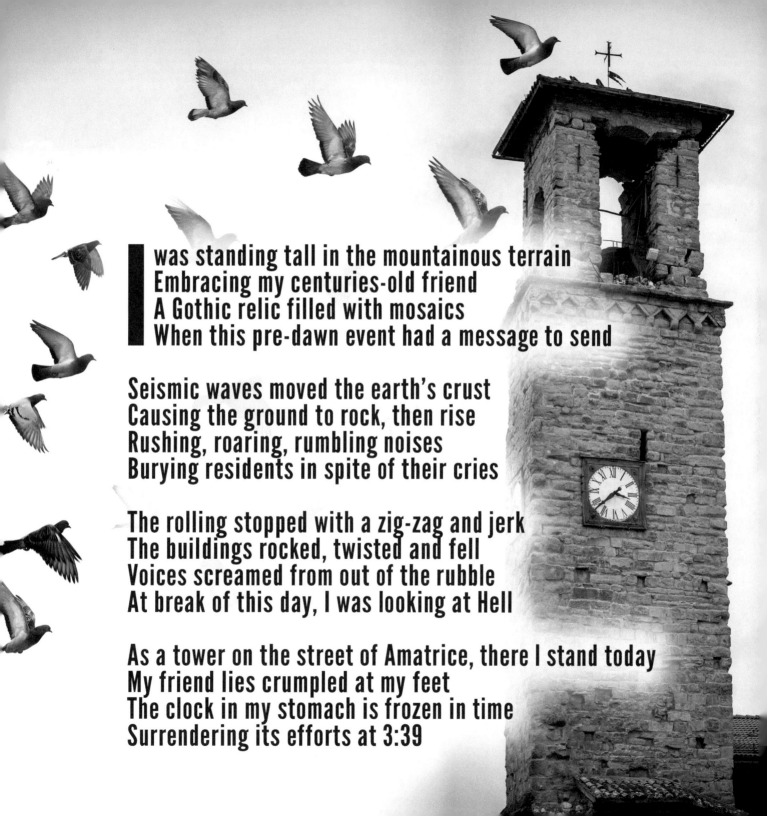

was standing tall in the mountainous terrain
Embracing my centuries-old friend
A Gothic relic filled with mosaics
When this pre-dawn event had a message to send

Seismic waves moved the earth's crust
Causing the ground to rock, then rise
Rushing, roaring, rumbling noises
Burying residents in spite of their cries

The rolling stopped with a zig-zag and jerk
The buildings rocked, twisted and fell
Voices screamed from out of the rubble
At break of this day, I was looking at Hell

As a tower on the street of Amatrice, there I stand today
My friend lies crumpled at my feet
The clock in my stomach is frozen in time
Surrendering its efforts at 3:39

eyes on the PRIZE

the waves are touching the shores of thought
Where dreams become reality
Words used to paint the pictures
Freeing the soul, it's needing to be

Celebrating the capacity for greatness
Inspiration spilling out, humbly obscure
Beautiful words meant to be said
Beautiful words meant to be read

Reaching for the incredible
Winning with indelible style
God put these dreams in me
And that's what God wants you to see

Shadow Love

Feeling love's afterglow
    Are reasons for the words
From a time of life on Oz
From a love that never was
Between the shadows and the soul

In that time of deep despair
Dancing with my memories
In a room, so cold and bare
The winged Cupid is not here
The final words remain unsaid
In this room along the track
The other heart's not coming back
In that fire across the sky
I feel a heart-beat, you and I
Now you are gone and I can see
The only one in love was me

TWILIGHT'S

His image endured triumphs and tragedy
This tall, gangly, goateed man
Seen in all the nooks and crannies
Way back when our country began
You know him by the clothes he wears
Swallow-tailed coat, tall top hat
You cannot miss the stars and stripes
The finger pointing like some aristocrat

LAST GLEAMING

Have you seen him slumped over?

With tears running down his face?

This patriotic emblem of our country

A country sometimes called a disgrace

He watches low-life vagrants

Wandering on our streets

Watches low-life bureaucrats

Rewarding those professional cheats

Is this your favorite uncle? The one that we love & call Sam?

Wearing the dazzling red, white and blue

A symbol of liberty for me and for you?

Valentine hearts trimmed with lace
Amazing moments we hold dear
A story that has no ending
A love that goes on when words disappear

When I laid my eyes on you
The room moved to another place
My heart beat fast and my spirit quickened
My world ascended into another space

Living with a love that is more than a love
A soul-mate is a gift from above
No heart was made for me like yours
With the touch of your hand, my spirit soars

Wonderful moments for eternity
Golden memories of just you and me
Magic that happened when we sang the same song
A melody finished when you came along

The
GARDEN

He walks along the graveled path
Beyond the hedgerow and the vine
Searching now his memories
To find some dreams he left behind
With silence wrapping hopes and fears
Remembering pain from those years

He feels the dampness of the ground
Embraces the stillness of the sound
Drawing a picture on the silence heard
Hearing then a quiet word
Coming from an empty space
Beautiful sounds he cannot trace
Succumbing now to his dreams
As the gift of holy streams
Here in a garden with stones and gnomes
Without the benefit of ahs and ohms
He found when left in deepest prayer
The Spirit of God was living there
A reminder today that God will speak
If in prayer His voice we'll seek

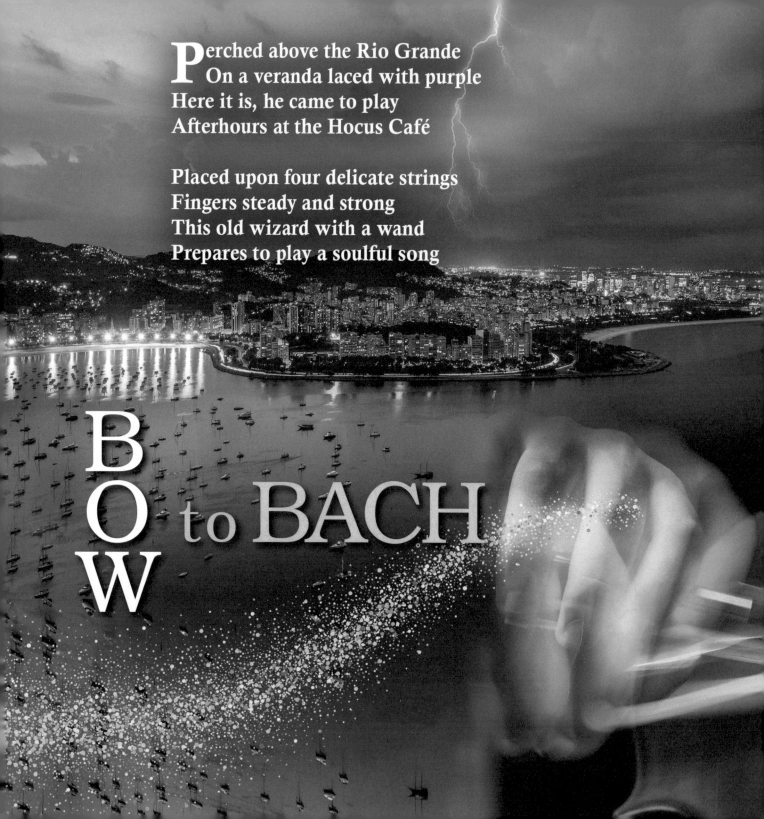

Perched above the Rio Grande
On a veranda laced with purple
Here it is, he came to play
Afterhours at the Hocus Café

Placed upon four delicate strings
Fingers steady and strong
This old wizard with a wand
Prepares to play a soulful song

BOW to BACH

Here in the outskirts of somewhere
His golden hair is damp with night air
His fingers now flying along the frets
The sounds from the cello are as good as it gets

Tantalizing sounds, lilting and wistful
Chords that hang and fade
Lifting the spirits, casting a spell
Glitter-dust wrapping a new jezebel

The sounds of the tones swell into the night
Through dark swaths of now shadowed silk
Reverberations splash from the riverbed
Bach's songs are sung without words being said

LAND of the DEAD

He walks in mud, sprouting up
Through the slimy sand
Wears a cloak draggling down
In a sunless land
This bearded man with a crooked nose
Operates a ferry-boat
Daily plodding through the mists
In the Land of the Dead on the River Styx

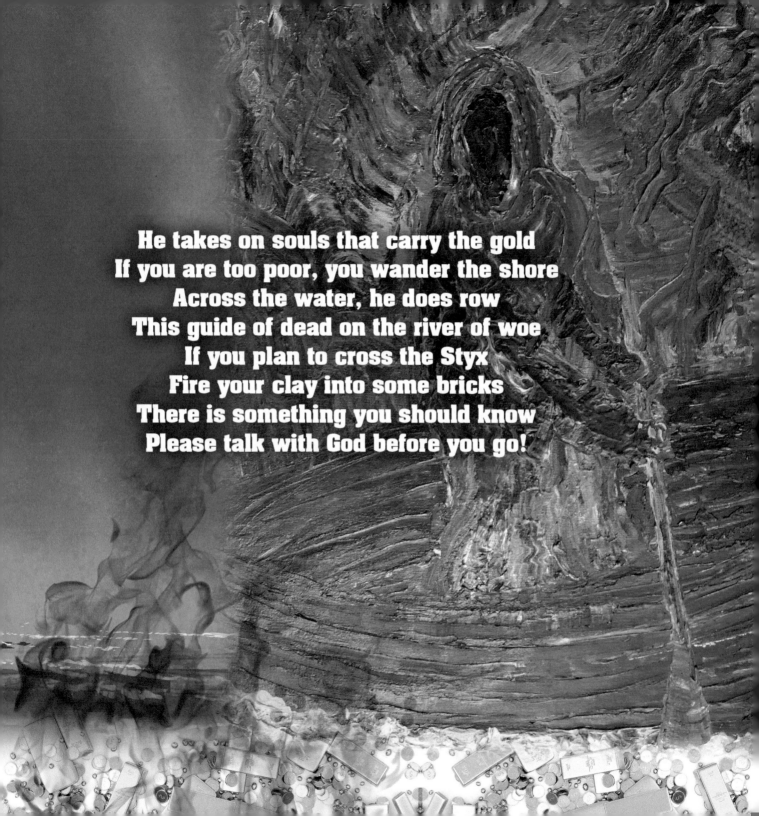

He takes on souls that carry the gold
If you are too poor, you wander the shore
Across the water, he does row
This guide of dead on the river of woe
If you plan to cross the Styx
Fire your clay into some bricks
There is something you should know
Please talk with God before you go!

NORTH POND HERMIT

With no destination, no map, no plan
Twenty-seven years of solitude began
Completely alone in the woods of Maine
Kissed by snow, the wind and the rain

He learned to walk from rock to root
Quietly seeking a cabin to loot
Satisfying his needs in every way
A secluded campsite for living each day

Born socially inept
Choosing to abandon the world
He found what he was looking for
By morphing into the local folklore

In this solitude with nature
He found a place so content
This hermit never lit a fire
Despite the coldness of the tent

He would steal propane tanks
Batteries, books, and food
Jeans, shirts and boots to wear
Things he needed while living there

His want to remain invisible
Many years later came to an end
When he triggered a planted wire
A wire with a message to send

This pale, bespectacled, middle-age man
Now lives with a brother where his life began
He stares at the sky, yearning to fly
This man is different in both mind and eye

It was summertime at the beach
  Worn-out planks on the old boardwalk
Breezes echoing off the dunes
An orchestra playing romantic tunes

Sounding rhymes in the summertime
Counting the stars in the sky
Knowing nothing of the hours or minutes
Beauty saturates her soul to the limits

SEASONS of SUMMER

Standing beneath shimmers of gold
The first glance probed her sensualities
Sending a river of pleasure
Where diving deep was hers to measure

Her mind was melting fast
As he returned that smile
His eyes were darker than the air
The summer's heat was everywhere

White linen trousers to match the washed clouds
Moving now to rhythms heard
A sensuous flash from below his chin
Where crisp autumn hair dusted his skin

To taste the salt from his lips
To feel the rhythms from his hips
A dream to fill a spinster's dream
While diving deep into another stream

Song of CREATION

Out in the world of the cosmos
Atoms dance producing a sound
Echoes from that invisible place
Holy streams from His heavenly face

A vast chorus in the sky
Singing the song of creation
Touching all beneath and around
Voices reaching souls with their sound

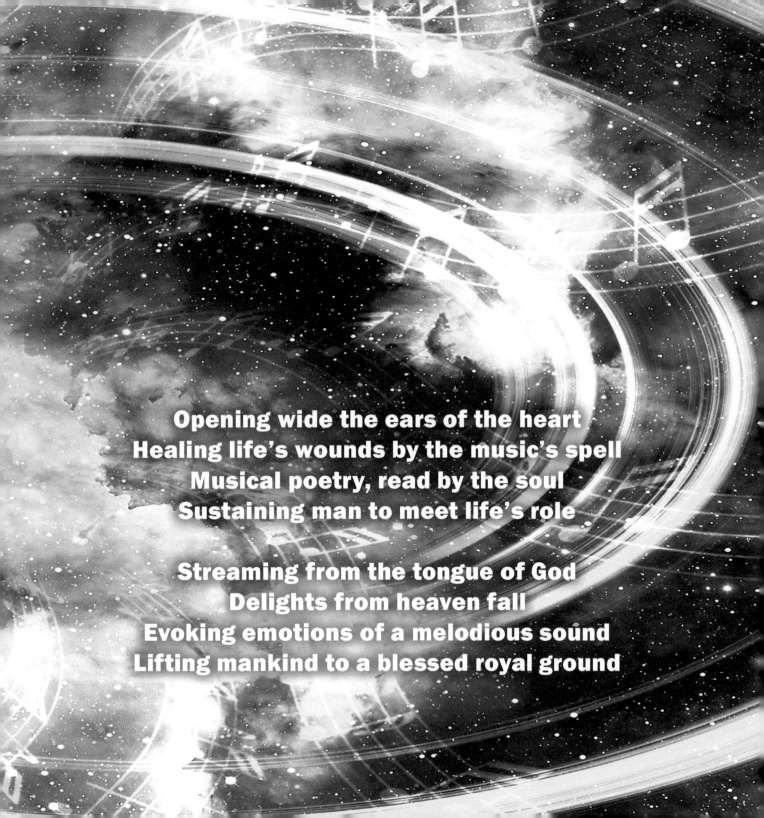

Opening wide the ears of the heart
Healing life's wounds by the music's spell
Musical poetry, read by the soul
Sustaining man to meet life's role

Streaming from the tongue of God
Delights from heaven fall
Evoking emotions of a melodious sound
Lifting mankind to a blessed royal ground

SUNKEN
City

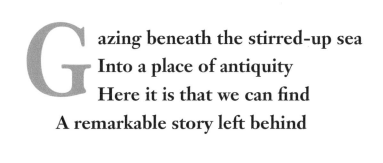

G azing beneath the stirred-up sea
Into a place of antiquity
Here it is that we can find
A remarkable story left behind

Where the river Nile and Mediterranean blend
In a criss-cross of canals
Thonis-Heracleion, a center for trade
Blossomed with ships heavily lade

Starring down for centuries
Colossal statues of granite red
A pharaoh, a queen, and a god called Happy
God of flooding, a symbol now dead

And, so it was, long ago
A city resting undisturbed
Until a shimmer caught a captain's eye
Centuries later, as he sailed by

WHEN

When we were young, back in the day
When dreams of the world were ours to play
We heard the sounds from the stratosphere
Felt the pulse when the sounds drew near

I remember being lost in song
Feeling the sparks ignite into flame
I loved you then, I love you still
Through today and tomorrow, I always will

Today when those sounds draw near
Fountains of tears swell from my heart
Your love is with me, I feel it today
Lingering still, though you went away

I have tears for you that will not die
I feel your presence filling the sky
I feel your unspeakable love
Descending with sounds that come from above

ECHOES OF FERRIDAY

Beneath the sodden, sultry moon
Amid the beer, sweat and rum
Unvarnished individuals polished their souls
In sanctified tones with a steady hum

The moments I spent in that place
Merging my soul while yet a child
My heart ached for what I could not name
My deepest longings were roaming wild

Red gum clapboards trimmed that space
Where Haney's Big House spilled its blues
Spilling the blue notes back in the day
Into the Mississippi and Ferriday

The music strains reached me there
Little by little showing my soul
My fingers doing what my mind desires
Running keyboards and lighting fires

dedicated to: Jerry Lee Lewis, Mickey Gilly, Jimmy Swaggart

REMINDER FOR MAN

The winds have begun to blow
Triple-crested waves of woe
Earthquake thunder and burning bolt
But looking high into the sky, I can see a bird afloat

It is the eagle who rises above the storm
It is the eagle who sets his wings
It is the eagle that soars with the wind
Above the world's pain and stings

Above life storms, we can see
God has a plan for you and me
His voice is sharper than a double-edged sword
The sound of the spirit, the voice of the Lord

Souls seek Him, souls wait
Our times are in God's hands
God's reminder for man to see
You won't be ashamed; if you wait for Me

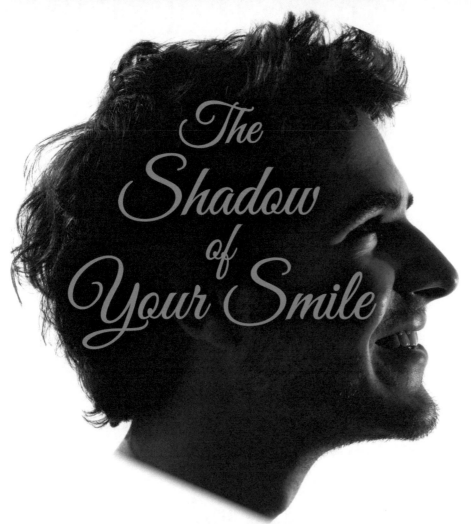

The Shadow of Your Smile

The air is warm and heavy
It is raining in my soul
I hear the rustle of leaves as I step
Remembering today that years take their toll
Pictures wafting in my mind
Awakened from a forgotten world
Steeping myself in yesteryears
With howling winds blowing burnt tears

From those days without a care
My mind sees him standing there
I sing about stars, far too high
Feel the rain drop from the sky
Beautiful words and melody
Coming from my heart
Remembering the love that it did bring
Long ago in that rapturous spring

Sojourn with me into the Arabian Desert
To the old place of Babylon
Meet my friends, Haban and Dakuri
Two nice men, who walk in a hurry

They have just finished a full week of labor
Received their pay in pieces of gold
Muggers are watching, so they don't want to lag
For the weight of the gold makes their pants sag

Just beyond the community spa
Their friend Duzi makes pottery vessels
Haban and Dakuri decide to stop
Would Duzi be able to store gold in his shop?

Duzi became a conniving vault-keeper
Vessels were filled at his fingertips
"Muahaha", he chuckled in private
While wringing his hands and licking his lips

Birth
of BANKING

"I will loan out many receipts
More than the gold that I store in my niche
Collect interest on all the new loans
No one's the wiser and I will get rich"

There in the ancient land of Babylon
The magic of money began
Led by this sick-twisted Robbing Hood
A Duzi born out of the Arabic sand

BANKING TODAY

Debt is where the problem lies
Citizens borrowing more and more
Interest rates artificially low
Causing the debts to grow and grow

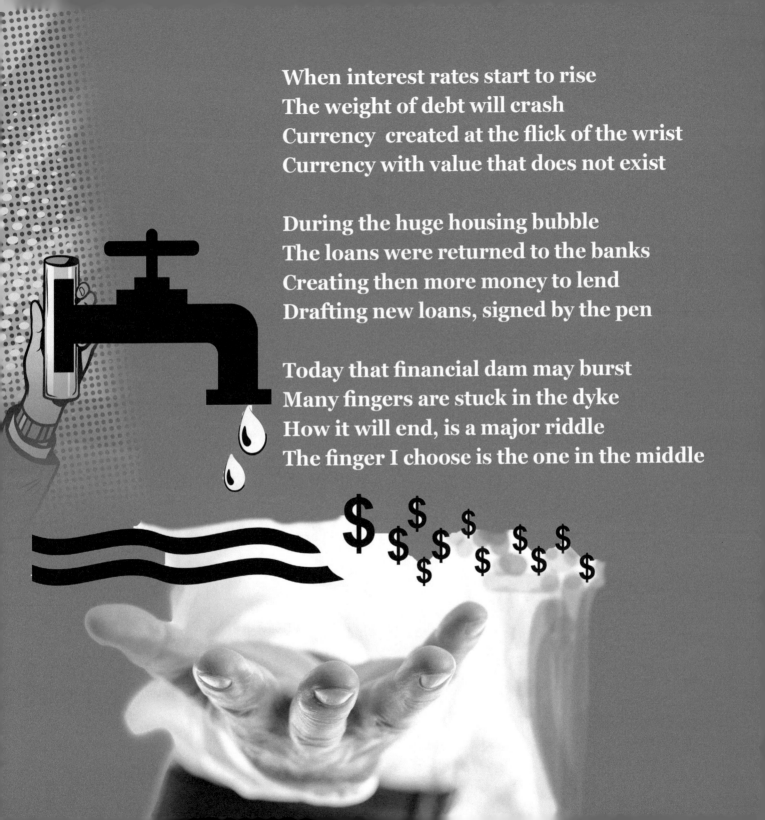

When interest rates start to rise
The weight of debt will crash
Currency created at the flick of the wrist
Currency with value that does not exist

During the huge housing bubble
The loans were returned to the banks
Creating then more money to lend
Drafting new loans, signed by the pen

Today that financial dam may burst
Many fingers are stuck in the dyke
How it will end, is a major riddle
The finger I choose is the one in the middle

WINTER

Here in the middle of nowhere
Sits a thatched cottage, pretty
Amid the backroads and winding ways
Near a small hilly town not far from the city
Today in the misty winter's sunshine
The smoke is curled and stirred
Rising through the violet hills
Draped with white to fight off the chills
The snow does begin to fly

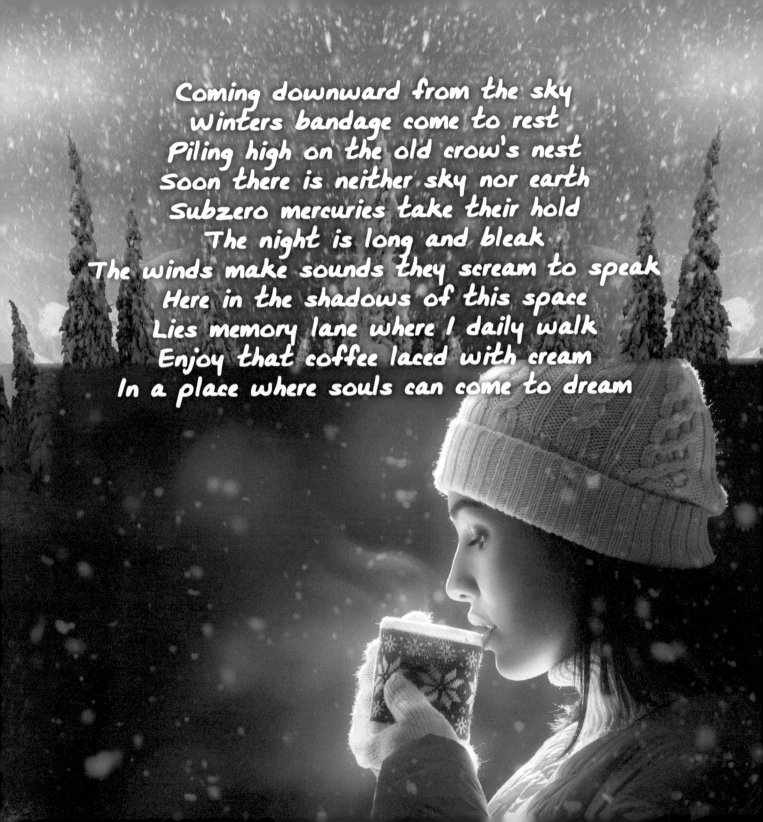

Coming downward from the sky
Winters bandage come to rest
Piling high on the old crow's nest
Soon there is neither sky nor earth
Subzero mercuries take their hold
The night is long and bleak
The winds make sounds they scream to speak
Here in the shadows of this space
Lies memory lane where I daily walk
Enjoy that coffee laced with cream
In a place where souls can come to dream

CAPTAIN

I am 19 years old
Critically wounded
Lying here in the jungle somewhere
The enemy fire is so intense
I know I can't get out of here

This day in Vietnam
MedEvac's are ordered to stay clear
We are out-numbered eight to one
 I tremble with great feelings of fear

My family is twelve thousand miles away
I shall never see them again
My world begins to fade in and out
When I hear the whirr of blades begin

Captain Ed Freeman, on a Huey
Had heard the radio call
Decided to fly in, no matter what
Loaded us up, 29 in all!

This Medal of Honor Recipient
Was wounded four times that day
We are hearing now, much later in time
That our hero Ed Freeman has just passed away

ED FREEMAN

ISLE of EIGG

On the western shore of Hebrides
Lays an ancient Eigg in the ocean breeze
With steep-sided lochs, bold and bare
Deep green waters, everywhere

An ancient Eigg, alive with two eyes
One eye seeing the future ahead
One eye reflecting thousands of years
A rich legacy, but one filled with tears

History takes them back
Fourteen hundred years
Through poverty, disease and massacre
Viking raids even deadlier

Today by an enchanted glen
A slim pillar of smoke ascends
Melting as the sunlight greets
Peace loving people on these streets

The days of torment are now gone
The families here sing a new song
Growing with life in everyway
The Isle of Eigg has new life in its sway

The magic is in the narrative
The tales I tell myself
But looking back I cannot find
What it was I left behind

Illusions of the future
Echoes of the past
Existing in the present
Where time is moving fast

That was then and this is now
Time designed what was meant to be
Like a spiral, it circled and quickened
Like great winds hitting the sea

Between the sunrise and the sunset
Life has been polished, then refined
Golden days with diamond rays
Replace the memories, we choose to erase
Making the present an unforgettable place

Jose, did you see by the dawns early light
What so proudly I mailed at the PO last night?
It was carefully wrapped and tied with a string
Overnight I was told for this package to bring

The mailman came by and the transport did fly
Express overnight to a USPS guy
Jose, did you get it? The carton I sent?
When you see your new gauchos, you'll know what I meant!

Oh yes, he received it
And fast I was told
He ripped open the wrapping
Like expecting some gold

Now strutting his stuff
In the mirror, you see
A sombrero, a mustache
And tight gauchos from Me

Handsome Jose

FLAMES
of THE
HEART

In a heart-beat, you and I
Were sending blazes to the sky
Our flames lit up the universe
With a fire without reverse
I did not want those flames to die
But heartbreak and heartache made me cry

Then flowing tears drowned the flame

While seeking solace for my pain

Without a word, without a thought

No hint of guilt for the pain you brought

Scattered fragments remain well hid

Of that sad dance that we once did

THAILAND ISLAND

Journey with me to Southeast Asia
Where forty-two Virgin Islands lay
Luring visitors to palm-fringed sands
Beyond where the tall-grass stands

The serpentine waterways weave their course
Through the tranquil forest
Until their glassy waters see
Limestone islands rise from the sea

Sitting amid emerald-green waters
Skeletons created from an acid rain
Fractured limestone beds
Pushing up their steep-sided heads

Here where white sand carpets stretch
Kissed by sea breezes blowing
Where the Earth was lifted from the sea
This world awaits our discovery

CRIES FROM

Everyone knows something is wrong
Our constitution is being shredded
A government born of the finest seed
Now based on money, profits and greed

Campaigns, cash and corruption
Shady characters on the go
For or against, lie after lie
Voices in America are now asking why

YELLOW EYES

Our Constitution was made for people with morals
A spiritual heritage handed down through the ages
Ideals echoed throughout those days
Brought forth successes in so many ways

We need to move up with eagle wings
See life from a broader prospective
Allow that eagle which flies through the skies
See restored country from his yellow eyes

We the People of the United States
in Order to form a more perfect
Union, establish Justice, en
domestic Tranquility, pr
the common defence, prom
general Welfare, and secu he
Blessings of Liberty to our lves
and our Posterity, do ordain and
establish this Constitution for the
United States of America...

HOLY BIBLE

MIDNIGHT TRAIN

Sitting in slippers

Pondering riddles of life

Wondering what gout is about

Finding my home when I do go out

My finest china is used everyday
Dispensable goods have been given away
I remember trips to unknown places
That game of poker and winning with aces
Tonight, I wait in the rain
Joining old folks on a midnight train
A train that is bound for a new destiny
On a track through a land I cannot see

ODIE

A fter a holiday weekend
I am picking up a load of mail
Huge bundles and packages
I shuffle the load, lean on the rail

Three steps down to the car
Is all I needed to peg
Next second I felt some very sharp claws
Piercing my jeans, going up my left leg

I dropped a couple of things
Made the sidewalk without fail
Managed to pull a kitten off
Opened my car door to unload the mail

When I slide inside
To take off down the road
Guess what is staring at me
From the other side of the load

That is where I made the decision
To take this Tabby home
Give him love and physical care
Comfort so he would not choose to roam

Odysseus is now his name
After the traveler from ancient Greek fame

Vibrations moving through the air
The sound of life is everywhere
There he sits straight and tall
Shoulders back against the wall
His sound engendered by dispersing a note
From a very old tune that another one wrote
Being in the moment, he reaches that spot
Mining his soul for the note that he sought
The song, the singer, passionately raw
Delivers a message, to ears filled with awe

OCTOBER'S CANVAS

As I walk through this changing time
Sunshine spreads a carpet gold
Purple threads trim the sky
October's beauty makes me cry

Bright red cones trim the trees
Jewels of autumn glowing
Treasured leaves laying down
Mists are rising from waters brown

Melting light, sighing winds
Cascading leaves from October trees
Walking a path of cobbled crust
Shed from life, filled with rust

There are reasons for the seasons
Turning leaves to red and brown
Autumn touches a sky of blue
When God paints a canvas for me and for you

Sitting beneath a dappled tree
Hearing sounds from the canopy
Searching the veils of misty clouds
His eyes reach for infinity

Then the sun slips the horizon
An invisible hand bends golden grass
Everything before him lined with gold
Shades of saffron begin to unfold

Bursts of gold on lavender melting
Clouds dropping from the sky
Past the touch and sight and sound
Moods are falling to the ground

So deep into the firmament he goes
White ragged wreaths cover the stars
A visionary now in ecstasy
Hears velvet footsteps by the tree

The Poet

Most blissful dream ever seen
That of being a poetry queen
From the depths of divine desire
Into a world with words on fire

Silent places where two worlds touch
The poet's pen and me
The winds quietly wave the trees
Rapturing words are found in the breeze

Queen

When I wander through
As most who dream are apt to do
No one sees my golden crown
Amid the orange and leaves of brown

Remembering those lonesome trees
The rhythmic songs they sang to me
Standing amid the sweeping plains
Kissed by water when it rains

Crownless though I remain
Walking through this still terrain
As I wait for another day
My chariot comes and we fly away

www.excursionsofthemind@gmail.com